THE
SOCIAL CONTRACT

The Hafner Library of Classics

[Number One]

THE
SOCIAL CONTRACT

BY

JEAN JACQUES ROUSSEAU

AN EIGHTEENTH-CENTURY TRANSLATION
COMPLETELY REVISED, EDITED,
WITH AN INTRODUCTION

BY CHARLES FRANKEL
Assistant Professor of Philosophy
COLUMBIA UNIVERSITY

1955

HAFNER PUBLISHING COMPANY · NEW YORK

Published at 31 East Tenth Street, New York 3, N. Y.

Printed in the United States of America

NOBLE OFFSET & PRINTING CO.
NEW YORK 12, NEW YORK

CONTENTS

THE SOCIAL CONTRACT

BOOK I

*Contains an inquiry why man passes from the state of nature
to the civil state, and what are the essential conditions
of the compact*

BOOK II

Treats of legislation

v

BOOK III

Treats of political laws, that is, of the form of government

BOOK IV

*In continuing to treat of political laws, the means of strengthening
the constitution of the State are pointed out*

INTRODUCTION

I

The Social Contract is a bible of contemporary politics. Like the Bible, Rousseau's treatise, it has been remarked, is more often talked about than read. Yet, like the Bible, it is responsible for much of the ceremonial of modern politics as well as for its moral and intellectual setting, and we are often unknowingly speaking its language and responding to its values. The terms and assumptions of *The Social Contract* are the common coin of political intercourse, and shape and limit political practice by providing the tools which we employ, consciously or unconsciously, to formulate social issues and to understand what we are doing. *The Social Contract* is not only an interpretation of political behavior. It is a pervasive aspect of the very behavior which is to be interpreted.

The Social Contract is the major source, for example, of the doctrine of popular sovereignty. <u>Popular sovereignty</u> is now more than a statement of fact or of ideals. To associate a political program with "The People" has become a kind of preliminary ritual without which the business of politics cannot be carried on. Almost all major modern states claim to be "People's States." Public deliberation, mass demonstrations, voting, and plebiscites are not only instruments for registering popular will but rituals for creating and arousing a popular will, and are as necessary to authoritarian states as to liberal ones. Few programs can expect success that do not use at least one such phrase as "People's War," "People's Peace," "People's Century," or "The Self-Determination of Peoples."

There is still another sense in which *The Social Contract* is a kind of secular bible. Practically all sides agree as to its truth or at least partial truth, or feel it best to pretend to do so; they disagree only as to its proper interpretation. The doctrine that the people are supreme now no longer clarifies issues so much as it incites some people to action against other people. Liberal democrats have been inspired by Rousseau's arguments for extending the opportunity to participate in public affairs to as many as possible, and lean upon his faith that the majority is more often right than wrong. Authoritarian *élites* have found support in Rousseau's admission that a minority may at times truly represent what the people really want, and have exploited Rousseau's principle that there is nothing self-contradictory in "forcing men to be free." Nationalists have taken a cue from Rousseau's doctrine that the State is a super-personality with a moral career of its own, that it is not simply a mechanism for satisfying certain human wants but is itself the very fulfillment of man's highest wants, incarnating the general will of the community and at once over-riding and gathering up all other interests.

For all these reasons, reading *The Social Contract* is like an adventure in the discovery of our political selves. Political habits, like other habits, have a way of coming to seem "natural" and inevitable. Reading *The Social Contract* brings our habits to life again by revealing them as the products, at least in this instance, of a conscious and considered choice. Our ways of behaving come to be seen as genuine options, as matters whose logic is to be explored and argued. In *The Social Contract* the "common sense" of politics today, its unspoken premises, its unconscious metaphors, are laid out before us for examination. One finds in it not only the words and conclusions that are on the surface of our discourse but the deeper meanings and assumptions which are, or ought to be, at the back of our minds.

II

Rousseau has held a curious fascination for the imagination of the western world because his systematic philosophy was also a personal confession, and his personal confession a type and symbol of universal history. What Saint Augustine has been to the Church, Rousseau has been to the modern State. These two men, so different in their historic roles and in the objects of their loyalties, were nevertheless strikingly similar in certain respects. Both had a way of converting events in their personal lives into symbols of universal experience. Augustine could see in a boyish prank a reflection of the universal malice of sin; Rousseau could turn a personal affront into a symptom of the organic disease of European society. Both wrote when ancient empires were collapsing, and both drew lessons which they turned to their own personal salvation. Both possessed a profound sense of their own sinfulness, though they knew that they shared the sinfulness of all men, and both were anxious for communion with others. Both were pursued by an intense consciousness of self which colored every experience and made them feel different from other men; yet both drew up programs for a transcendent form of social organization with a moral and corporate personality of its own, in which men might lose their willful individuality by freely consenting to a higher will in which all men share. *General Will*

There is of course a connection between any philosopher's individual temperament and what he has to say about the public world. But in Rousseau it was a matter of principle to say nothing about the public world which he had not accredited in the privacy of his heart. Rousseau was one of those personalities that seem to have no surface. Nothing with him could be merely skin-deep. No event, no idea, no disagreement with others, was so small that it might not involve his entire personality and the entire external structure of society. No public event was so great that he might not take it as a personal challenge.

In other men this constitutional incapacity or unwillingness to distinguish between the large and the small, or to set a boundary between themselves and the outer world, might seem morbid, petty, or egotistical. Certainly Rousseau's insistence on taking everything personally and on taking his personality for everything irritated and provoked many of his contemporaries, as it has irritated and fascinated many of those who came later. Rousseau, who felt himself to be fundamentally simple and affectionate, succeeded in arousing the personal animosity of almost all his eminent contemporaries, and his life was a series of friendships that turned into enmities. Indeed, his *Confessions* suggest that towards the end of his life he had come to believe that he was the object of an organized conspiracy.

Yet those who knew him could not escape the suspicion that there was something original and important about the man, and later generations, while they have not been able to agree as to what he said, have had to recognize that his saying it has made a tremendous difference. No other figure with the exception of Voltaire moved his generation so, or had so much to do with bringing the next generation together for revolutionary action. It is indeed difficult to say that Rousseau had no sense of proportion, because the proportions he gave to his experience do not now seem to have been an over-estimate. His self-expression has become public property in education, morals, politics, and art, and the dimensions of his personality have become a kind of standard of normality if not of health.

The divergent streams which Rousseau's influence has taken provides one of the fascinating episodes in the history of ideas. Robespierre's rationalistic Cult of the Supreme Being had sources in Rousseau; yet Rousseau's attack upon intellectual analysis isolated from genuine emotion, and his faith in the immediate insights of sentiment and feeling, stimulated romantic intuitions of realities higher than any which mere reason alone might grasp. Rousseau's sense of being different was one source of the romantic cultivation of idiosyncrasy, and his life-long struggle with himself provided a model for the many affected and disaffected heroes of nineteenth-century poetry and politics who made an agonized and divided conscience a sign of distinction. Yet Rousseau sentimentalized homely, everyday virtues and glorified the simple untutored instincts of plain men, peasants, villagers, and artisans. His feeling that the nearer opinions approach unanimity, the greater is the dominance of the general will, became an argument for faith in the commonplace and gave new dignity to the tyranny of "public opinion." Rousseau's spirit moves not only in the Bohemias of romantic individualists but along Main Street: Stendhal's Julien Sorel found inspiration in Rousseau; but the uniformity of the stifling Philistines of Flaubert's Yonville also draws on elements in Rousseau, even though he himself was thinking of the virtues of an agrarian rather than a bourgeois, community.

It has therefore been tempting to say that Rousseau's thought is a mass of willful inconsistency and unorganized eclecticism. Undoubtedly there is much in Rousseau that seems to warrant the divergent interpretations that have been placed upon what he had to say. But Rousseau himself seems to have believed that in general his ideas were held together if not by cold-blooded logic then by an internal continuity of perspective and feeling, a higher dialectic of sentiment. For later generations it is as though the several phases of his personality, which had a kind of dynamic unity in his own eyes, have broken apart from each other and become separate philosophies. The unity in Rousseau is the unity of things felt deeply by the same heart and seen intensely from a single center of vision. In his case more perhaps than in any other, his ideas must be understood in the context of his unifying personal experience.

Jean-Jacques Rousseau was born in Geneva in 1712. From the beginning, as he reports in his *Confessions*, he seemed marked for misfortune. Rousseau's mother died in giving him birth, and his father "was ever after inconsolable," nor could he ever embrace Jean-Jacques "but the sighs, the convulsive pressure of his arms, witnessed that a bitter regret mingled itself with his caresses." The infant's health was poor and it was to remain poor all his life. He inherited only one of all the gifts that had been bestowed on his parents, "a feeling heart," and even this "feeling heart," which had been the source of his parents' felicity, was to be, as he later discovered, the source of all his misfortunes.

Rousseau's early life was unsettled, and he moved frequently from place to place and from trade to trade. It was in Paris, where he lived continuously from 1744 to 1756, that Rousseau found his vocation and his ideas took shape. But Rousseau did not reach Paris until his thirtieth year, and he joined the advanced intellectual circle of Grimm and Diderot as a self-taught man. Though he established his reputation in Paris, Rousseau was incapable of becoming a Parisian. As he confessed, he always felt out of his element there. The more he found the mannered formalities of the Parisian *salon* oppressive, the more he nostalgically idealized the simple honesty of manners at Geneva. The conversation of the *salon*, the politely shocking epigrams, the frivolous dialectical twists, the books written in public, all repelled Rousseau. The continual talk about civic virtue seemed cold and hypocritical, and the freedom of Parisian life seemed licentious to a man brought up in austerely Calvinist Geneva.

Not only did Rousseau feel awkward socially, but he was by all his deepest inclinations a solitary man who found social life a distraction and who worked best when he was left alone. It was this strain in his nature which perhaps more than any other perplexed and estranged men like Diderot. Society, as Diderot phrased it, was for the philosopher a divinity on earth. The *philosophes* found it difficult to understand how a philosopher, a man devoted to the improvement of society, could be so unsociable, or how he could think about society without being willing to live in it. Nor could they understand how he could find stimulation in any way but through the daily exchange of ideas. It was perhaps this failure of sympathetic imagination in the *philosophes*, and what seemed to Rousseau their complementary lack of personal independence, that first made him distrust them.

Above all, Rousseau never found it easy to enjoy the life of a professional intellectual. He was sickened by the constant analysis of human emotions and values in which the Parisian intellectuals indulged. He was shocked especially by what he took to be the systematic expression of intellectualism, the philosophic materialism of men like Holbach, and the systematic egoism of Helvetius, which reduced human behavior to the collision of material particles in a void. Rousseau found it difficult to believe that anyone could seriously pretend to divorce his mind from his feelings so completely as to be willing to argue that all human behavior was the clash of competing egoisms in a moral void.

Undoubtedly Rousseau missed some of the point and some of the flavor of the radical philosophy. In the first place, systematic materialism in metaphysics and morals was an extreme view which was not widely shared. More important, Rousseau did less than justice to the emancipating impact of the new theories on the supernatural philosophy and clerical politics of the *ancien régime*. He took materialism at its word, its first word, and he failed to see the disinterested devotion that was at its core. Indeed, he failed to see through the sceptical mask of the *philosophes*, and to detect in their opposition to enthusiasm their own enthusiastic piety towards nature and zealous charity towards men, which, for example, informs the closing pages of Holbach's *System of Nature*.

But very often the persistent materialistic analysis of human behavior is, in conversation especially, merely a disguised and intellectualized form of gossip. Many of those who frequented the *salons* found in the new philosophy simply a chance to gossip abstractly, to degrade systematically human motives and actions. As one of the ladies of the *salon* is said to have remarked, "Helvetius had told everybody's secret." Like these others, Rousseau looked upon the new philosophy as gossip, but unlike these others he refused to be either amused or instructed. His "feeling heart" responded primarily to the emotional tone of intellectualism. The response was often injudicious

and massive; but it led to an intuition that cut beneath the usual distinctions between radical and conservative, believer and unbeliever. Rousseau came to believe that in the general absence of conscience, affection, and emotional vitality, the new philosophy had simply erected materialism, selfishness, and calculation into principles. Thus, what in appearance was the most radical attack upon the *ancien régime* was at bottom only a product and a reaffirmation of the qualities in that society which had thwarted men's instincts for loyalty.

Rousseau's feelings were expressed in the essay which first established him as an intellectual himself, the *Discourse on the Arts and Sciences*, which was followed a few years later by the *Discourse on the Origin of Inequality*. Though Voltaire called these essays Rousseau's two attacks upon the human race, and though they seem superficially opposed to the belief expressed in *The Social Contract* that the social order is sacred and basic to everything else, it seems probable that they were not contrary to the views expressed in *The Social Contract*. Rousseau's *Discourse on Political Economy*, which was written about the same time as his *Discourse on the Origin of Inequality*, contains the rudiments of most of the views expressed in *The Social Contract*, and indicates that Rousseau did not change his mind radically between his earlier essays and his later works. The "society" which Rousseau criticized in his early pieces is not the "society" he praised in *The Social Contract:* the one is a pseudo-society built on selfishness and calculation, the other is a genuine community built on spontaneous love of country. In his earlier essays it is likely that Rousseau had the image of Parisian society with its sophisticated display in his mind's eye, and that the word "society" carried some of the connotations which now attach to it when it is used on the "society page" of a daily newspaper. In *The Social Contract* Rousseau seems to be thinking of his idealized Geneva, which he saw in the pattern of the Platonic city-state.

In 1756, Rousseau left Paris for the solitude of the country. A series of literary works issued from his retreat, culminating in 1762 in the appearance of Rousseau's two major works, *The Social Contract*, and a treatise on education, *Emile*. The publication of these books immediately upset all Rousseau's plans for a quiet life. Within a month after its publication *Emile* was condemned at Paris, and the man who once characterized himself as the only man in France who believed in God was forced to flee the defenders of religion. He took refuge in Switzerland, but even this country did not offer a permanent refuge. His native city Geneva, in what must have been a crowning blow, condemned not only *Emile* but *The Social Contract* as well, and issued a warrant for Rousseau's arrest if he entered Genevan territory. Other cities in Switzerland followed Geneva's lead, and Rousseau was forced to spend the next four years as a refugee moving from place to place.

Largely in the effort to defend himself against the attacks upon him, Rousseau began during these years the series of works of self-explanation and justification which finally led to his *Confessions*. His writing during this period oscillated strangely between the position, maintained with quiet self-assurance and acute dialectic, that his persecution was an incident in the working of impersonal social forces, and the increasingly morbid conviction that he had been singled out for persecution. On the one hand, he responded to the action of his native city by formally renouncing his citizenship, and in his *Letters from the Mountain* he wrote a dignified and probing analysis of the recent history of Geneva in which his own persecution appeared as but an incident in a larger pattern of oligarchic repression of the democracy. On the other hand, Rousseau made less and less of a secret of his growing conviction that the pretended friends of liberty, led by Voltaire, were plotting against him and had repeatedly betrayed him to the authorities.

In 1766, Rousseau was offered refuge in England by David Hume. Rousseau was acclaimed in England, and Hume seems to have been at first very much taken with his guest. But it was only a few months before the two men quarreled. In 1767, Rousseau left England, and in 1770, he finally returned to Paris, where he lived until his death in 1778. In 1794 the new French Republic honored him as a national hero and removed his body to the national shrine.

III

A contemporary reader may find it difficult to understand the revolutionary influence attributed to *The Social Contract*. Despite Rousseau's statements elsewhere that exclusively analytic methods have only a limited use, the argument follows an almost geometrical line. Rousseau makes very few compromises with any limitations of interest or education on the part of his readers. A large part of the book revolves around the technical problems traditional among political philosophers, and Rousseau's language for dealing with these issues is neither new nor conspicuously "emotive." In addition, there is much that seems ambiguous and even contradictory, the terms Rousseau uses are often vague, and the argument is undeniably abstract and difficult to apply to specific cases.

Nevertheless, the impact of the book is unmistakable. It is not only the passage of time that gives *The Social Contract* its dynamic power to awaken men out of the sense that whatever is, is inevitable. Other books that have been written to accomplish a program which was subsequently to become more or less a matter of course frequently have this effect upon later generations of readers. But in its own day *The Social Contract* achieved this effect in an especially heightened way because it was written by a man for whom moral choice and moral freedom were matters of acute and constant concern. What most immediately appealed to Rousseau's generation was his insistence that men's social arrangements are the products of human choice, and that men must bear the moral responsibility for the kind of society they construct or accept. Carrying Rousseau's induplicable personal accent, *The Social Contract* was an incitement to revolution because it did what a revolutionary book has to do: it joined justice and utility, and showed men that their interest and their duty were on the same side. *The Social Contract* made social change not only a matter of self-interest but a moral obligation incumbent upon all.

It appeared under the most propitious circumstances for making its ideas seem clear. The idea of the general will provided a unifying symbol which joined the scattered discontents of men of different classes and gave a name and a philosophical basis to the general opposition to the worst abuses of the Bourbon regime. However general the language, it was difficult for men who wished the government to serve their interests, and who were supporting it with loans and taxes, not to give a very concrete application to passages like the following:

> We are told that a despot ensures civil tranquillity for his subjects.
> Be it so; but what do his subjects gain if the wars which his am-

bition draws them into, if his insatiable avarice, and the vexations of his administration, desolate the country even more than civil dissensions? What do they gain if this very tranquillity is one of their miseries? We find tranquillity also in dungeons; but is that enough to make them enjoyable?

To men who were tired of the internal disputes that divided the ruling classes, the dominance of the general will seemed to promise an end to factionalism and the emergence of a more generous kind of mutual understanding and concern for the good of all.

> So long as several men unite and consider themselves as one body, they have but one will, which is to promote the common safety and general well-being. While this union continues, all the springs of the State will be vigorous and simple, the maxims by which they are regulated will be clear and comprehensible; and there will be no jarring, opposing interests; the common good will then be everywhere evident, and nothing will be necessary but a sound understanding to perceive it. For peace, union, and equality are enemies of political subtleties.

Simpler men who were irritated by the elaborate dialectic of apologists for the *ancien régime* found in the general will an instrument for reducing public affairs to more generally comprehensible terms; middle-class people who were restive under the social distinctions that separated them from the nobility found in the general will a demonstration of their own dignity and superior political intelligence.

> Men of integrity and simplicity are difficult to deceive because of their very simplicity: lures and refined pretexts do not impose upon them, and they have not even cunning enough to be dupes. When we see, among the happiest people in the world, groups of peasants directing affairs of State under an oak, and always acting wisely, can we help but despise the refinements of those nations which render themselves illustrious and miserable by so much art and mystery?

In particular, Rousseau's inference that government is simply the servant of the people stirred those who were opposed to the existing regime, while, to its defenders, it seemed to undermine the very foundations of civil order. *The Social Contract* went so far in affirming the obligations of government to the people that, to those in power, it seemed to leave the governed with no obligation at all to obey their government, and to be simply an open invitation to recurrent revolution. The censorship of Rousseau's native city correctly appraised the revolutionary force of Rousseau's tract and paid it its proper tribute:

> In *The Social Contract*, the author, after having derived the author-ity of governments from the purest sources, after having success-fully displayed the immense advantages of the civil state over the state of nature, soon restores all the disorders of this primitive state; the laws that constitute any government seem to him to be always revocable, and he does not see any reciprocal obligation between those who govern and those who are governed; the former seem to him only instruments that the people can always change or crush at will. . . . He considers all forms of government to be only provisional, experiments that can always be changed. . . .[1]

IV

The Social Contract was an incident in the history of politics, but it was also a commentary upon that history, intended to throw light upon the particular circumstances of eighteenth-century Europe by relating them to more lasting aspects of the political process. Neither in Rousseau's mind nor in fact was the book simply a tract for the times. It was also a conscious philosophical work in which Rousseau used contemporary experience to lead him to principles of the most general application and in which he used these general principles to understand and criticize existing practices.

In pursuit of such principles Rousseau to a very large extent used the language traditional among political philosophers. But Rousseau's transforming personal vision and experience gave new content to the most conventional terms. The idea of a social contract as the basis of social obligation and social organization, for example, was the conventional point of departure for secular political philosophy in Rousseau's day. As used by modern philosophers, the social contract was a device for exhibiting the implicit logic upon which social relations were based. By the technique of contrasting social behavior with a "state of nature" in which there was no agreement to live socially,

---

[1] *Conclusions de M. le procureur général Henri-Robert Tronchin sur le* Contrat social *et l'*Emile *de Rousseau;* in E. Dreyfus-Brisac, ed., *Du Contrat social* (Paris, 1896), appendix XI, pp. 421–422.

philosophers hoped to bring out the peculiar nature and function of social organization and to provide a basis for the authority — or for limitations on the authority — of government. This appeal to a social contract was not in the main speculative history. Only rarely was the "state of nature" or "the social contract" intended to refer to actual historic events. The men who used these ideas were not attempting to write history but philosophy, and wished to delineate principles which would show the rationality of social arrangements or exhibit the unjustifiable irrationality of existing societies.

But if the social contract did not have an historical reference it nevertheless involved certain assumptions which gave a peculiar twist to speculation on the principles of politics. By contrasting social organization with an imaginary state of nature, social-contract theory tended to establish a dichotomy between "the individual" and "society," and to argue as though social organization was by the very fact of being *social* a restraining force which could only be justified on grounds of necessity. Social-contract theory assumed the individual human being to be equipped with a complete set of interests or rights apart from society, and attempted to give a moral justification for society in primarily individualistic terms. Furthermore, the idea of the social contract, especially as developed by Thomas Hobbes, tended to base social morality mainly upon prudence: men were "obliged" to obey social authority only because it was a better safeguard on the whole for interests which they already had.

The title of Rousseau's book might well give the impression that his treatise is simply a further elaboration of these reigning preconceptions. In fact, it is anything but this. The very title, *The Social Contract*, is something of a misnomer. The social contract is not only relegated to a minor role in Rousseau's argument, but what there is left of it is so substantially reinterpreted as not to be recognizable as a contract at all. Rousseau, whose master in political philosophy was Plato, was in fundamental disagreement with the individualistic premises of social-contract theory. He did not think that the peculiar rationality of social obligation could be explained in terms of an agreement between individuals who, in isolation from one another, were nevertheless complete men, nor did he regard prudence as a sufficient basis for moral obligation. Rousseau disagreed further with the prevalent conviction that the moral authority of society rests upon natural rights that have validity outside any kind of social organization. By "natural rights" Rousseau meant rights realized only in and by a society. They were "natural" because they represented the fuller realization of human nature. Society was for Rousseau not an "aggregation" of individuals but an "association," a way of speaking which was intended to communicate the fact that when individuals act as a group new dimensions of behavior appear. For Rousseau, living in society represented the triumph of interests that were distinctively different from, and more completely human than, merely individual interests.

In short, Rousseau used the phrase, "the social contract," not primarily for purposes of philosophic analysis but as a way of dramatizing the moral situation implicit in the individual's living in society. Set against the backdrop of an imaginary "state of nature," the distinctive quality of social relations as alone providing the basis for *moral* action emerges more clearly, and the principles which distinguish a justifiable society — that is, a true society — are highlighted. "The passing from the state of nature to the civil state produces in man a very remarkable change, by substituting justice for instinct in his conduct, and giving to his actions a moral character which they lacked before."

But the use of the social contract in this way means that it is not really a contract at all. A contract implies mutual promises, and the undertaking by each of the contracting parties of obligations which will satisfy some existing interest of the other party to the contract. Rousseau's "social contract," however, is the exchange of a situation in which there is no human morality for one in which there is. It actually creates obligations and interests which did not exist before, and obligates the individual to a social whole, or to his own mandatory general will, against which he has no reciprocal claims. Such a situation may or may not be intelligible, but it can hardly be called a contract. Indeed, since Rousseau political thought has moved away from the social contract and closer to the classic Greek insistence that the community is the teacher of virtue, and that only in the community is human behavior or morality possible or even definable.

The modern theory of the social contract was employed to explain and justify the sovereignty of the national state. The idea of sovereignty — of the absolute supremacy of the State over all other forms of social organization — was developed as a tool in the struggle of national monarchies to subordinate the feudal Church and baronial classes, and has been central in the political philosophy of modern times. The problem of sovereignty includes two questions which are often confused and which are not easily separable. in practice, but which are nevertheless logically distinct: (1) the question as to which power or group of powers is actually supreme in a society, and whether such supremacy is absolute; and (2) the advantages and disadvantages of maintaining within any society an ultimate authority for pronouncing the last word in disputes among individuals and groups. The first emphasizes political issues, the second legal issues.

In Rousseau's background Hobbes was the outstanding representative of the attempt to base legal sovereignty on the actual facts of political power, while John Locke on the whole made the attempt through the mechanism of natural rights and popular consent to establish a political power whose moral authority rested on grounds other than mere power. Rousseau's theory of sovereignty grew out of the attempt to combine the advantages of both these approaches. With Locke he was convinced of the principle that might alone does not make right, and of the need to limit the powers of government, to make it responsible to some law or principle beyond itself. On the other hand, he was convinced with Hobbes that morality has no meaning or basis outside a society. In particular, Rousseau was convinced that there was a fundamental truth in Hobbes' insistence that law without the ability to enforce obedience is not law at all but merely wishful talk.

Rousseau's theory of sovereignty, however, was not an eclectic one with no distinct principles of its own. To Hobbes he responded quite justly that a contract made by men in which they agree to subject themselves to an external supreme power is not a contract at all. There were, indeed, certain considerable difficulties within Hobbes' theory, cogent and forceful as it was. Is the strongest power strongest because all men mutually agree to obey it? Or do all men mutually agree to obey it because it is in fact the strongest power? If it is the latter alternative, then there seems to be no sense in speaking of a contract since men would perforce have to obey anyway. If it is the former alternative, however, and if the sovereign is rendered supreme only by virtue of everybody's agreeing to recognize its supremacy, then it is those who originally make the agreement who in fact are the supreme power in the community. And if this is true, it seemed incredible to Rousseau that those who hold this power should give it up without qualification or condition. Sovereignty cannot in fact be transferred, and no "contract" can make whoever or whatever is supreme in the community inferior.

Such considerations led Rousseau to his theory of popular sovereignty. He was convinced that, as a matter of right, any pact of subjection, any agreement that one man or group of men has a right to command others, is but an acceptance of slavery and is without moral justification; and he was convinced that, as a matter of fact, the power of any particular group within the community is not absolute but rests at least to some extent upon the consent of other groups, and is, therefore, relative, contingent, and transitory.

Consequently, Rousseau was led to ask, "Where does sovereignty in the sense of absolute power and ultimate moral authority actually reside?" His answer was that it can only reside in the people as a whole. If no body of men within the State holds absolute power, then absolute power must rest with the entire community. Rousseau's theory of sovereignty thus represents a departure in one fundamental respect from the theories of his predecessors. Sovereignty for him does not reside in any particular group. The government cannot be sovereign, as Hobbes argued, because its power is conditional. It cannot even be sovereign under the limitations of a secondary contract with the community, as Locke had suggested: a contract made between the supreme community and the government is meaningless because the community cannot be compelled to maintain the conditions of the contract against its will.

But in another respect Rousseau retained a major preconception of the philosophic tradition concerning sovereignty. He could find no particular group that was absolutely supreme: this might have led him to the conclusion that absolute sovereignty was a meaningless or false conception. Instead he continued to assume that society was in fact a unity and that absolute sovereignty referred to something genuine. Consequently, if sovereignty resided nowhere in particular, it must be everywhere all at once and reside in the community as a whole. This is not an easy position to understand or to apply. If some ultimate authority is being sought to pronounce the last word in the solution of conflicts within the community it is not much help to argue that this authority is the community as a whole, or to suggest that a community in which there is division is not really a community at all.

Why, indeed, should one assume that the community or "the people" are in fact a unitary whole? With the exception of small city-states, the will and the power of the entire community is never concretely present in any public assembly. As a rule the people do not exercise power directly but through deputies, through particular men; and Rousseau was acutely sensitive to the fact that such men often develop special interests that are not in accord with those of the rest of the community. And even within the small city-state, where all the citizens legislate, the community splits up into parties, factions and classes. How may the position be maintained that sovereignty resides in the body of the people taken as a unit?

It was in wrestling with these problems that Rousseau introduced his most distinctive conception, the idea of the general will. There is, he argued, within any community a will for a collective good which is something over and above the partial, private ends which individuals in the society, merely as individuals, may desire. This general will is to be kept sharply distinguished from what the members of a society may, by majority vote or even by unanimous agreement, decide is their good. Such a decision, which Rousseau distinguished from the general will by calling it "the will of all," may be wrong. The general will, by definition, cannot be wrong because it is the very standard of right. The general will was thus a device for bringing together in the theory of sovereignty the two emphases upon power and upon right. In the general will we find the ultimate source of sovereign power and the ultimate criterion of sovereign authority.

The general will is something over and above the sum of all the individual wills present in the society, but it is not something completely apart from individuals. Each individual has both a private will, in which he isolates his desires from the social group within which they function, and a general will, in which his individual desires are at the same time the desires proper to his status as a member of society and a citizen. Each individual has the responsibility as a citizen to act in accordance with his general will rather than in accordance with his private will, just as it is the major function of those who are entrusted with public power to evoke and to obey the general will. It is the fact that the general will is not apart from individuals but resident in them, while at the same time it is something over and above their wills merely as individuals, that makes it possible for Rousseau to resolve what he considers the major problem of political philosophy: "Where shall we find a form of association . . . by which every person, while uniting himself with all, shall obey only himself, and remain as free as before?" What, in other words, is the principle of political right?

Many of the fundamental problems of contemporary democracy grow out of the fact that in part democracy involves the attempt to apply ideals developed in the intimate community-life of the Greek city-state to an era of vast nation-states, highly centralized government, and technical specialization. Rousseau himself was aware of these problems and of the difficulty of establishing an absolutely best form of government valid for all conditions. But as a moralist he was predominantly concerned with the principles of political right, and his analysis of politics was complicated by the fact that he recurrently criticized existing conditions in the light of principles that grew out of his nostalgic idealization of ancient city-states and his own city of Geneva. Probably the idea of the general will seemed to have some concrete embodiment to Rousseau, who was pre-occupied with the city-state as a form of government. Yet, as Rousseau himself realized, the city-state was on the whole an anachronism, and the attempt to apply conceptions like the general will to more complex conditions only enhanced the verbal and ambiguous character of the theory.

In general, most of the problems present in the theories of his predecessors, and which he criticized, are resolved on one level by *criticisms* Rousseau's theory, but reappear on the new level of the general will. How can we tell when the general will is being realized? What are the marks which indicate that a particular decision, or a particular group, do in fact represent the general will of the community? Rousseau's distinction between the "general will" and the "will of all" means that the majority on any issue need not be right or "general," and that we cannot depend on majority decision or on a utilitarian counting of noses to determine the public good. A minority, as

Rousseau admits, may be the true representative of the general will, and indeed, if it does represent the general will, to assert itself over the majority is not only permissible but obligatory. This is the theory on which contemporary authoritarian parties have often functioned. On the other hand, Rousseau also suggests that as differences become fewer and unanimity is approached the general will is made more evident — a view that can be used to justify majority oppression of the few who may continue to differ from the majority.

It is indeed very difficult to know exactly what Rousseau did mean by "the general will." Rousseau had set out to establish a principle of political right which would combine the merits of the Hobbesian emphasis upon power with the Lockeian emphasis upon government based on consent and moral authority. By showing that supreme power and supreme moral authority were unified in the conception and the exercise of the general will, Rousseau hoped to remove the separation in previous political theories, and, more important, in existing social practice, between governor and governed, and between might and right. The general will was proposed as the answer to the question, "How can a man be free while he is subject?"

If, however, the general will is not necessarily realized in any actual society, then it may be regarded as an ideal norm. But if it is merely an ideal norm, Rousseau has erected a moral criterion which is separated from the necessity for actual power — a view which is incompatible with the political realism of Hobbes with which Rousseau was deeply impressed, and which he wished to maintain in his own theory. On the other hand, if the general will is not only an ideal standard but a description of an existing state of affairs, then it seems fair to ask where it resides, and how we know that all individuals within a nation have the same general will or that they are all really members of the same society.

One cannot escape the suspicion, in view of the various and even contradictory applications which Rousseau himself made of the idea, that he may have meant several things by "the general will," and that when he came to apply the idea to concrete cases he often wavered between interpreting it as an abstract ideal and as a description of an existing state of affairs. Actually Rousseau's doctrine seems to warrant almost anything from complete justification of the *status quo* to a state of permanent revolution. If, for example, the general will is interpreted as absolutely supreme in fact, then any government must by necessity be under its control, and consequently justifiable. This is of course a conclusion which Rousseau wished to avoid, although later conservative and idealist theorists made much of it. But Rousseau took a burden upon himself which was not really incumbent upon him in the light of his critique of social-contract theory. Since Rousseau did not really regard social organization as "unnatural" it was not necessary for him to give a wholesale justification of society in general, but only to develop principles which would help distinguish between good and bad societies. This was undoubtedly his principal intention. Nevertheless, he differed so completely from the individualistic premise of social-contract theory that society is by its nature a restraining force that he apparently felt called upon to give an absolute answer on the other side. Consequently, at times he resolved the problem of how men may be subject while remaining free by denying the existence of any genuine constraint in society. This is reflected in his famous dictum that men may be forced to be free: even the convict is free in the sense that he is imprisoned by his own general will that men who follow their private wills in the way he has shall be punished. From this point of view, whenever the individual differs from the community he is private, wrong, and enslaved; whenever his individual will is unified with that of the community he is general, right, and free. Thus the problem of the irresponsibility of the absolute sovereign in Hobbes' philosophy recurs in Rousseau in the shape of the irresponsibility of the community or nation, and the "general will" provides a justification for what some critics have called "an orgy of fraternity." For if it is impossible for one's *real* will to be in disagreement with the community, then clearly the community can do no wrong.

On the other hand, when he employs the general will as a disembodied ideal, Rousseau appears to emphasize the fact that no form of government but direct democracy in which every citizen participates in the business of government is absolutely justifiable. Any other form of government — and Rousseau admits that direct democracy is for the most part impracticable — is only second-best, because it involves the establishment of a body of officials who will sooner or later tend to develop at the expense of the community their own special and private will as a distinct group. Consequently revolu-

similarity to marx revolution

tion — that is, the destruction of government and the recapturing of power by the sovereign community under the direction of the general will — is recurrently justifiable. It is this view of government which is in the background of many anarchist doctrines of the nineteenth century, and which contributes to the Marxist doctrine of "the withering away of the State."

Much of Rousseau's analysis of the general will seems indeed so abstract and general that practically anything seems to follow from it. In the last analysis, the general will seems to be simply each man's will to be general. Kant's conception of the rational will as the will to act so that one's action may be taken as a universal rule of conduct is the formal development of Rousseau's general will.

There is, however, still another interpretation of the general will which need not reduce it to a purely formal conception without content. When the general will is taken to stand for something static and finished, either a perfect ideal or a completely realized state of affairs, most of the problems we have been discussing occur. But the will to be general also had for Rousseau a much more lively and immediate significance, and the general will may be viewed as the name for a specific kind of personal and social process or trend. Rousseau was not incapable of abstractions, but there were few abstractions which were not also ways of describing immediately felt responses to experience. Rousseau's "general will," if interpreted in the light of his revulsion against the divided and insulated society of Paris, connotes a specific kind of demand made upon his experience, a demand for the elimination of barriers to shared experience and for a public life that would be more generally accessible to men. It is enlightening to consider Rousseau's conception of the general will against the background of his *Emile*, which appeared in the same year as *The Social Contract*. A dominant principle in the education of Emile, as Rousseau prescribes it, is to avoid any clash of personal wills. If, for example, the boy is in the habit of breaking windows he will be placed in a windowless room, and it will be pointed out to him impersonally, almost casually, that he is being placed there not because any person is angry with him but simply in order to protect windows. Emile will learn by being confronted with the impersonal (or "natural") consequences of his behavior rather than with its impact on other people's arbitrary passions.

The *Emile* may provide a clue to what Rousseau thought it felt like to have a general will. To will to be general meant to unify one's will with others, which can only be accomplished when other wills are also so disposed. The good society in which the general will is made concrete will be one in which individuals are most complete and most "natural," that is, released from the arbitrary restraints placed upon their growth and their communion with others by their own partially developed wills or by the merely personal preferences of others.

In the context of Rousseau's general philosophy and personal experience the general will may be taken to refer to a direction or process of experience, a persistent demand that social life be less divided. In this sense the general will appears prophetic of that process by which men's opportunities to be general and to participate knowingly and actively in affairs that have public value might become progressively less impeded by external obstacles of class or religious creed or insularity. Rousseau emerges as the evoker of the democratic vision of a society which, in Lincoln's phrase, "progressively lifts the weights from the shoulders of men." Seen in this light, the "community" is not something already or permanently realized, but an ideal to be pursued and a quality of experience to be recurrently enjoyed when men are engaged with one another fraternally.

Rousseau is the pre-eminent spokesman for the values of equality and fraternity. No more than any other values are these absolute and self-justifying; as sympathetic critics of democracy like Tocqueville and Mill have pointed out, equality and fraternity may under certain conditions constitute genuine menaces to liberty and individual diversity. But equality and fraternity may also be the conditions for the positive freedom involved in the larger realization of individual potentialities, and Rousseau is the source of this revised and enlarged conception of freedom as an ideal to be progressively realized by positive social action. Rousseau was a critic of values; but his great power was as an originator who evoked the peculiar savor and feel of new values, and brought home to men that equality and fraternity, though they might not be unmixed goods, were nevertheless goods and brought an added dimension to experience. He speaks in all those for whom co-operation among equals is not only a mechanism of social action but a quality of life to be enjoyed for its own sake.

NOTE ON THE TRANSLATION

This translation of *The Social Contract* is based on an anonymous translation published in London in 1791. The work carried the following preface:

> The high honours which have been recently paid to the memory of Rousseau by the National Assembly of France, avowedly from a persuasion that a treatise of his, entitled *Du Contrat Social*, had prepared the way for the Revolution which has lately taken place in that country, must naturally excite a desire in the minds of Englishmen to be acquainted with a work which could lay the foundations of so important an event. A translation is therefore offered to the public, in which care has been taken to give the sense of the author in the plainest language, that all who choose to trace in this treatise the principles of the new system of French government may do so, without that difficulty which is sometimes found in reading translations of philosophical works.

The translation has been extensively revised to eliminate inaccuracies, and the spelling has been modernized, but an effort has been made to retain its distinctive virtues as a translation which is close in time and spirit to the original eighteenth-century political tract.

The notes of the present editor are enclosed in brackets.

THE
SOCIAL CONTRACT

OR

PRINCIPLES OF POLITICAL RIGHT

By J.-J. ROUSSEAU

CITIZEN OF GENEVA

Fœderis æquas
Dicamus leges.
　　Virgil, *Aeneid*, XI

FOREWORD

THIS LITTLE TREATISE is extracted from a much more extensive work, undertaken without consulting my abilities, and laid aside long ago. Of the passages which could be selected from what was written, the following are the most considerable, and appear to me to be the least unworthy of being offered to the public. The rest is already destroyed.

BOOK I

My design in this treatise is to enquire whether, taking men such as they are, and laws such as they may be made, it is not possible to establish some just and certain rule for the administration of the civil order. In the course of my research I shall endeavour to unite what right permits with what interest prescribes, that justice and utility may not be separated.

I shall enter on my enquiry without saying anything about the importance of my subject. If I am asked whether I am a prince or a lawgiver, that I write on politics, I shall answer that I am neither, and for that reason I am a political writer. If I were a prince or a lawgiver, I should not waste in theory the time which I ought to employ in practice; I would act or I would remain silent.

Born a citizen of a free State, and, as such, a member of its Sovereign, however weak the influence of my voice may prove in the determination of public affairs, the right of voting on such occasions imposes on me the duty of informing myself on the subject: and I am happy, whenever I meditate on governments, to find that my researches always afford me new reason to admire that of my own country.

CHAPTER I

Subject of the First Book

Man is born free, and yet we see him everywhere in chains. Those who believe themselves the masters of others cease not to be even greater slaves than the people they govern. How this happens I am ignorant; but, if I am asked what renders it justifiable, I believe it may be in my power to resolve the question.

If I were only to consider force, and the effects of it, I should say, "When a people is constrained to obey, and does obey, it does well; but as soon as it can throw off its yoke, and does throw it off, it does better: for a people may certainly use, for the recovery of their liberty, the same right that was employed to deprive them of it: it was either justifiably recovered, or unjustifiably torn from them." But the social order is a sacred right which serves for the basis of all others. Yet this right comes not from nature; it is therefore founded on conventions. The question is, what those conventions are. But, before I come to that point, I must establish the principles which I have just asserted.

CHAPTER II

Of the First Societies

THE EARLIEST and the only natural societies are families: yet the children remain attached to the father no longer than they have need for his protection. As soon as that need ceases, the bond of nature is dissolved. The child, exempt from the obedience he owed the father, and the father, from the duties he owed the child, return equally to independence. If they continue to remain together, it is not in consequence of a natural, but a voluntary union; and the family itself is maintained only by a convention.

This common liberty is a consequence of the nature of man. His first law is that of self-preservation, his first cares those which he owes to himself; and as soon as he has attained the age of reason, being the only judge of the means proper to preserve himself, he becomes at once his own master.

It appears therefore that families are the first models of political societies: the chief represents the father of the family, the children the people; and being all born equal, and all free, they in either case only alienate their liberty in order to obtain what is more useful. All the difference between the two societies is that, in the family, the gratification which paternal tenderness derives from a consciousness of benefiting those who are the objects of it makes a full amends to the father for the care he bestows on the children; while, in the State, the pleasure of commanding takes the place of that love which the chief does not feel for his people.

Grotius denies that all human power is established for the benefit of those who are governed; and he instances slavery in proof of his assertion.[1] But his constant manner of reasoning is to establish right by fact.[2] A more satisfactory mode might be employed, but none more favourable to tyrants.

It is therefore doubtful, according to Grotius, whether the whole human race belongs to about one hundred men, or this hundred men to the human race; and he appears throughout his book to incline to the former opinion, which is also the idea of Hobbes: so that, according to them, mankind is divided into herds of cattle, each herd having its master who protects it in order to devour it.

As the herdsman is of a nature superior to that of his cattle, so the herdsmen of men, that is, their chiefs, are of a nature superior to their people. So reasoned, according to Philo's account, the Emperor Caligula, who concluded very justly from analogy that either kings were gods, or men were beasts.

The reasoning of Caligula comes to just the same point as that of Grotius and Hobbes. Aristotle had said, before any of them, that men are not naturally equal, but that some are born for slavery and others for dominion.[3]

Aristotle was right; but he mistook the effect for the cause. Nothing is more certain than that all men who are born in slavery are born for slavery. Slaves become so debased by their chains as to lose even the desire of breaking from them; they love their servitude, even as the companions of Ulysses loved their brutishness.[4] If there are some who are slaves by nature, the reason is that men were made slaves against nature. Force made the first slaves, and slavery, by degrading and corrupting its victims, perpetuated their bondage.

I have not said anything of King Adam, or Emperor Noah, the

---

[1] [Grotius (1583-1645), *De jure belli ac pacis* (*The Law of War and Peace*), Bk. I, chap. 3. This book, published in 1625, was a pioneer in the development of the idea of an international law governing the relations of sovereign states. It also did much to formulate the conception of "natural law" as distinct and separate from "theology."]

[2] "Learned studies of public right are often only the history of past abuses; and it is foolish and stubborn to take the trouble to study them too deeply." (*Essay on the Interests of France in Relation to its Neighbours*, by the Marquis d'Argenson.) This is precisely what Grotius did.

[3] [Aristotle *Politics*, Bk. I, chap. 2.]

[4] See a short treatise by Plutarch entitled *That Animals Use Reason*.

father of three great monarchs, who parted the universe among them, like the children of Saturn, whom they are by many supposed to be. I expect to be applauded for this moderation; because, as I am descended in a direct line from one of these princes, and perhaps from the eldest branch, who can tell whether, in the verification of titles, I might not find myself the legitimate king of the human race? However it be, we can discover nothing but that Adam was sovereign of the world, as Robinson Crusoe was of his island, because he was its only inhabitant; and the happiest circumstance attending the empire was that the monarch was secure in his throne, having nothing to apprehend from rebellions, wars, or conspiracies.

CHAPTER III

Of the Right of the Strongest

THE STRONGEST are still never sufficiently strong to ensure them continual mastership, unless they find means of transforming force into right, and obedience into duty. Hence the right of the strongest — a right which seems ironical in appearance, but is really established as a principle. But shall we never have an explanation of this term? Force is a physical power; I do not see what morality can result from its effects. To yield to force is an act of necessity, not of inclination; or it is at best only an act of prudence. In what sense then can it be a duty?

Let us suppose for a moment the existence of this pretended right. I see nothing that can arise from it but inexplicable nonsense. For, if we admit that force constitutes right, the effect changes with the cause: all force which overcomes the first succeeds to its right. As soon as men can disobey with impunity, they can do so justifiably; and because the strongest is always in the right, strength is the only thing men should seek to acquire. But what sort of right is that which perishes with the force that gave it existence? If it is necessary to obey by force, there can be no occasion to obey from duty; and when force is no more, all obligation ceases with it. We see, therefore, that this word "right" adds nothing to force, but is indeed an unmeaning term.

If in saying, "Let us obey the powerful," they mean to say, "Let us yield to force," the precept is good, but it is superfluous, for it never is or can be violated. All power, we are told, comes from God. I grant it does; but all diseases likewise come from the same hand, and yet who ever forbade us to call in a physician? If a robber surprises me in a corner of a wood, is it necessary that I should not only give him my purse when forced to do so, but am I in conscience obliged to give it to him, though I should be in a position to escape? For the fact is, the pistol which he holds is also a power.

We must grant, therefore, that force does not constitute right, and that obedience is only due to legitimate powers. Thus everything goes back to my first question.

Might doesn't make right

CHAPTER IV

OF SLAVERY

SINCE NO MAN has any natural authority over his fellows, and since force produces no right to any, all justifiable authority among men must be established on the basis of conventions.

If an individual, says Grotius, can alienate his liberty, and become the slave of a master, why may not a whole people alienate theirs, and become the subject of a king?[1] There are some equivocal words in this sentence, which require an explanation; but I will confine myself to the word "alienate." To alienate is to give or sell. But a man who becomes the slave of another, cannot give but must sell himself, at least for a subsistence. But for what do a people sell themselves? A king, so far from furnishing his subjects with subsistence, draws his own from them; and, according to Rabelais, a king does not subsist upon a little. Do subjects therefore give their persons on condition that the prince will condescend to accept their property also? I see nothing, after such a gratuity, that there remains for them to preserve.

We are told that a despot ensures civil tranquillity for his subjects.

[1] [*Loc. cit.*]

Be it so; but what do his subjects gain if the wars which his ambition draws them into, if his insatiable avarice, and the vexations of his administration, desolate the country even more than civil dissensions? What do they gain if this very tranquillity is one of their miseries? We find tranquillity also in dungeons; but is that enough to make them enjoyable? The Greeks enjoyed the same kind of tranquillity while they were shut up in the cave of the Cyclops, and were expecting every moment that it would be their turn to be devoured.[1]

To say that a man gives himself gratuitously is absurd and incomprehensible; such an act is unjustifiable and void, because the person who performed it is not in his proper senses. To say the same of a whole people is to suppose the people are all mad; and folly does not make it right.

If each individual could alienate himself, he could not alienate his descendants; for, being born men and free, their liberty is their own, and no person can dispose of it but they themselves. Before they arrive at the age of reason, the father may, in his children's name, stipulate conditions for their preservation and welfare, but not give them up irrevocably, and unconditionally; for such a gift would be contrary to the designs of nature, and exceed the rights of paternal authority. It would therefore be necessary, in order to make an arbitrary government justifiable, that each generation should be at liberty to admit or reject it: but then such a government would not be arbitrary.

To renounce our liberty is to renounce our quality of man, and with it all the rights and duties of humanity. No adequate compensation can possibly be made for a sacrifice so complete. Such a renunciation is incompatible with the nature of man; whose actions, when once he is deprived of his free will, must be destitute of all morality. Finally, a convention which stipulates absolute authority on one side, and unlimited obedience on the other, must be considered as vain and contradictory. Is it not clear that there can be no obligation to a person from whom everything may be justly required? And does not the single circumstance of there being no equivalence and no exchange also annul the act? For what right can my slave have against me,

---

[1] [Compare Locke, *Of Civil Government*, chap. 18, where the same scene from the *Odyssey* is used.]

since everything that he has belongs to me, and, his right being mine, this right of mine against myself is absolute nonsense?

Grotius and others derive from war another origin for this pretended right of slavery. The victor having, according to them, a right to kill the vanquished, the latter may purchase his life at the expense of his liberty; a convention which is so much the more justifiable because it tends to benefit both parties.[1]

But it is clear that this pretended right of killing the vanquished results not in any manner from the state of war; because, while men remain in their primitive independence, there is no intercourse between them sufficiently settled to constitute either peace or war; and they are not naturally enemies.[2] It is a concurrence of things, and not of men, that occasions war; and the state of war cannot rise out of simple personal concerns, but only out of real relations; nor can private war between man and man exist either in the state of nature, where there is no settled property, or in a civil state, where everything is under the authority of the laws.

Private combats, duels, and rencontres are acts which do not constitute a state of war; and with regard to the petty wars authorized by the "Establishments" of Louis IX of France, and suspended by the Peace of God, they were abuses of the feudal government, a system so completely absurd that it contradicted the principles of natural right and of every sound polity.

War is therefore not a concern between man and man but between State and State, in which individuals are only enemies accidentally, not as men, or as citizens, but as soldiers; not as members of a country, but as its defenders. In fine, States can only have other States, and not men, for enemies, because there can be no true relation between things of different natures.

This principle is conformable to the established maxims of all times, and the invariable practice of all politically organized peoples. Declarations of war are not so much to inform the powers as their subjects. The stranger, be it a monarch, a private individual, or a whole people, that robs, kills, or detains the subjects of another prince, without

---

[1] [Grotius, *Op. cit.*, Bk. III, chap. 7.]

[2] [Compare, for example, Hobbes, *De Cive*, preface, and *Leviathan*, chap. 13, where the state of nature is said to be a state of war, "where every man is enemy to every man." This is the position with which Rousseau is here taking issue.]

previously declaring war against that prince, is not an enemy but a robber. Even in real war, a just prince, while he carries away whatever he can seize upon in an enemy's country that belongs to the public, respects the persons and property of private people, because he respects the right by which he holds his own. The end of war being to subdue the hostile State, the army of one State has a right to kill the defenders of the other while they have arms in their hands; but, as soon as they lay them down and surrender themselves, they cease to be enemies or the instruments of enemies; they become simply men, and the victors have no longer any right over their lives. Sometimes it may be possible for one State to destroy another State without destroying one of its members: and war does not give a right to do anything beyond what is absolutely necessary to its end. These are not the principles of Grotius, neither are they adopted on the authority of the poets; but they are derived from the nature of things, and founded on reason.

With regard to the right of conquest, it has no other foundation than the law of the strongest. If war does not give the conqueror the right to massacre the conquered, then that right does not exist and cannot serve as a basis for the right to enslave the conquered. Men have no right to kill the enemy but at the time when it is impossible to enslave them; the right of enslaving cannot therefore be derived from the right of killing: it is therefore an iniquitous barter to make them purchase, at the price of their liberty, that life over which the conquerors have no right. In establishing the right of life and death on that of slavery, and of slavery on that of life and death, is it not clear that we become involved in a vicious circle?

But supposing that this terrible right of massacring everybody did exist, the slaves made in war, or a conquered people, could be bound by no obligation at all to their master, and would only obey him while they were compelled by force to do so. In taking his service as an equivalent for sparing his life, the victor confers no favour on the man he has vanquished: instead of killing him — from whence he could derive no advantage — he spares him that he may reap the fruits of his labour. So far, therefore, is the conqueror from having acquired, by saving the life of the conquered, any other authority over him to second that of force, that the state of war continues to subsist between them as formerly, and even their union is the effect of it; and, while the rights of war are exercised, no treaty of peace can be supposed to exist. I shall be told perhaps that they have made a convention. Be it so; but this convention is so far from terminating the state of war that it supposes the continuance of it.

Thus, in whatever light we view things, the right of slavery is found to be null, not only because it is unjustifiable but because it is absurd and has no meaning. The terms "slavery" and "right" contradict and exclude each other. Be it from man to man, or from a man to a people, it would be equally nonsensical to say: I make a covenant with you entirely at your expense, and for my benefit; I will observe it as far as my inclination leads me, and you shall observe it as far as I please.

There is no right of slavery

CHAPTER V

That We Must Always Go Back to a First Convention

Had i granted all which I have refuted, the favourers of despotism would not have found their cause advanced by it. There will always be a great difference between subduing a multitude and governing a society. When unorganized men[1] are successively subjugated by one individual, whatever number there may be of them, they appear to me only as a master and slaves; I cannot regard them as a people and their chief; they are, if you please, an *aggregation*, but they are not as yet an *association;* for there is neither public property, nor a political body, among them. A man may have enslaved half the world, and yet continue only a private individual; his interest is separate from that of others, and confined to himself alone. When such a man falls, his empire remains unconnected and without any bond of union, as an oak dissolves and becomes a mass of ashes when consumed by fire.

An association exists when there is public property or political body

"A people," says Grotius, "can give themselves to a king."[2] According to Grotius, then, they are a people before they give themselves to a king. The donation itself is a civil act, and supposes a public

[1] [*des hommes épars*.]

[2] [*Op. cit.*, Bk. I, chap. 3.]

consultation. It would therefore be better before we examine the act by which they elected a king, to enquire into that by which they became a people; for that act, being necessarily anterior to the other, is the true foundation of society.

In fact, if there was no prior convention, where would be — unless the election was unanimous — the obligation which should bind the minority to submit to the choice of the majority? And whence would a hundred men, who wish to submit to a master, derive the right of binding by their votes ten other men who were not disposed to acknowledge any chief? The law which gives the majority of votes the power of deciding for the whole body can only be established by a convention, and proves that there must have been unanimity at one time at least.

CHAPTER VI

OF THE SOCIAL COMPACT

I WILL SUPPOSE that men in the state of nature are arrived at that crisis when the strength of each individual is insufficient to overcome the resistance of the obstacles to his preservation. This primitive state can therefore subsist no longer; and the human race would perish unless it changed its manner of life.

As men cannot create for themselves new forces, but merely unite and direct those which already exist, the only means they can employ for their preservation is to form by aggregation an assemblage of forces that may be able to overcome the resistance, to be put in motion as one body, and to act in concert.

This assemblage of forces must be produced by the concurrence of many; but as the force and the liberty of each man are the chief instruments of his preservation, how can he engage them elsewhere without danger to himself, and without neglecting the care which is due himself? This difficulty, which leads directly to my subject, may be expressed in these words:

"Where shall we find a form of association which will defend and protect with the whole common force the person and the property of each associate, and by which every person, while uniting himself with all, shall obey only himself and remain as free as before?" Such is the fundamental problem of which the Social Contract gives the solution.

The articles of this contract are so unalterably fixed by the nature of the act that the least modification renders them vain and of no effect; so that they are the same everywhere, and are everywhere tacitly understood and admitted, even though they may never have been formally announced; until, the social compact being violated, each individual is restored to his original rights, and resumes his native liberty, while losing the conventional liberty for which he renounced it.

The articles of the social contract will, when clearly understood, be found reducible to this single point: the total alienation of each associate, and all his rights, to the whole community; for, in the first place, as every individual gives himself up entirely, the condition of every person is alike; and being so, it would not be to the interest of any one to render that condition offensive to others.

Nay, more than this, the alienation being made without any reserve, the union is as complete as it can be, and no associate has any further claim to anything: for if any individual retained rights not enjoyed in general by all, as there would be no common superior to decide between him and the public, each person being in some points his own judge, would soon pretend to be so in everything; and thus would the state of nature be continued and the association necessarily become tyrannical or be annihilated.

Finally, each person gives himself to all, and so not to any one individual; and as there is no one associate over whom the same right is not acquired which is ceded to him by others, each gains an equivalent for what he loses, and finds his force increased for preserving that which he possesses.

If, therefore, we exclude from the social compact all that is not essential, we shall find it reduced to the following terms:

Each of us places in common his person and all his power under the supreme direction of the general will; and as one body we all receive each member as an indivisible part of the whole.

From that moment, instead of as many separate persons as there are contracting parties, this act of association produces a moral and collective body, composed of as many members as there are votes in the assembly, which from this act receives its unity, its common self, its life, and its will. This public person, which is thus formed by the union of all other persons, took formerly the name of "city,"[1] and now takes that of "republic" or "body politic." It is called by its members "State" when it is passive, "Sovereign" when in activity, and, whenever it is compared with other bodies of a similar kind, it is denominated "power." The associates take collectively the name of "people," and separately, that of "citizens," as participating in the sovereign authority, and of "subjects," because they are subjected to the laws of the State. But these terms are frequently confounded and used one for the other; and it is enough that a man understands how to distinguish them when they are employed in all their precision.

CHAPTER VII

OF THE SOVEREIGN

IT APPEARS from this formula that the act of association contains a reciprocal engagement between the public and individuals, and that each individual, contracting, as it were, with himself, is engaged under a double character; that is, as a member of the Sovereign engaging

---

[1] The true sense of this word is almost entirely lost among the moderns: the name of "city" is now generally used to signify a town, and that of "citizen" applied to a burgess. Men do not seem to know that *houses* make a "town," but that *citizens* make a "city." The Carthaginians once paid dearly for a mistake of this kind. I have never seen it mentioned that the title of *cives* was ever given to the subjects of any prince, not even to the Macedonians formerly, or to the English at present, although they are nearer liberty than any other people. The French alone use the name of "citizen" familiarly to all, because they have no true idea of it, as appears from their dictionaries; and without knowing its meaning they are in danger of falling into the crime of lèse majesté, by usurping a title to which they have no just claim. The word "citizen" with them means a virtue, and not a right. Bodin made a very gross mistake, when, in speaking of "citizens" and "burgesses," he mistook the one for the other. M. D'Alembert was better acquainted with the meaning of these terms, and in his article "Genève" he has very properly marked the difference between the four orders of men — indeed I may say five, by including the foreigners — which are found there, and of which two orders only compose the republic. No other French author that I know of has comprehended the true sense of the word "citizen."

with individuals, and as a member of the State engaged with the Sovereign. But we cannot apply here the maxim of civil right, that no person is bound by any engagement which he makes with himself; for there is a material difference between an obligation to oneself individually, and an obligation to a collective body of which oneself constitutes a part.

It is necessary to observe here that public deliberation, which can bind all the subjects to the Sovereign, in consequence of the double character under which the members of that body appear, cannot, for the opposite reason, bind the Sovereign to itself; and consequently that it is against the nature of the body politic for the sovereign power to impose on itself any law which it cannot break. Being able to consider itself as acting under one character only, it is in the situation of an individual forming a contract with himself; and we see therefore that there neither is nor can be any kind of fundamental law obligatory for the body of the people, not even the social contract itself. But this does not mean that this body could not very well engage itself to others in any manner which would not derogate from the contract; for, with respect to what is external to it, it becomes a simple being, an individual. But the body politic, or the Sovereign, which derives its existence from the sacredness of the contract, can never bind itself, even towards outsiders, in anything that would derogate from the original act, such as alienating any portion of itself, or submitting to another Sovereign. To violate the contract by which it exists would be to annihilate itself; and that which is nothing can produce nothing.

As soon as this multitude is united in one body, you cannot offend one of its members without attacking the body; much less can you offend the body without incurring the resentment of all the members. Thus duty and interest equally oblige the two contracting parties to lend aid to each other; and the same men must endeavour to unite under this double character all the advantages which attend it.

Further, the Sovereign, being formed only of the individuals who compose it, neither has, nor can have, any interest contrary to theirs; consequently, the sovereign power need give no guarantee to its subjects, because it is impossible that the body should seek to injure all its members; and we shall see presently that it can do no injury to any individual in particular. The Sovereign, by its nature, is always everything it ought to be.

But this is not so with the relation of subjects towards the Sovereign, which, notwithstanding the common interest, has nothing to make them responsible for the performance of their engagements if some means is not found of ensuring their fidelity.

In fact, each individual may, as a man, have a private will,[1] dissimilar or contrary to the general will which he has as a citizen. His own private interest[2] may dictate to him very differently from the common interest; his absolute and naturally independent existence may make him regard what he owes to the common cause as a gratuitous contribution, the omission of which would be less injurious to others than the payment would be burdensome to himself; and considering the moral person which constitutes the State as a creature of the imagination, because it is not a man, he may wish to enjoy the rights of a citizen without being disposed to fulfil the duties of a subject. Such an injustice would in its progress cause the ruin of the body politic.

In order, therefore, to prevent the social compact from becoming an empty formula, it tacitly comprehends the engagement, which alone can give effect to the others — that whoever refuses to obey the general will shall be compelled to it by the whole body: this in fact only forces him to be free; for this is the condition which, by giving each citizen to his country, guarantees his absolute personal independence, a condition which gives motion and effect to the political machine. This alone renders all civil engagements justifiable, and without it they would be absurd, tyrannical, and subject to the most enormous abuses.

CHAPTER VIII

Of the Civil State

THE PASSING from the state of nature to the civil state produces in man a very remarkable change, by substituting justice for instinct in his conduct, and giving to his actions a moral character which they lacked before. It is then only that the voice of duty succeeds to

[1] [volonté particulière.]
[2] [intérêt particulier.]

physical impulse, and a sense of what is right, to the incitements of appetite. Man, who had till then regarded none but himself, perceives that he must act on other principles, and learns to consult his reason before he listens to his inclinations. Although he is deprived in this new state of many advantages which he enjoyed from nature, he gains in return others so great, his faculties so unfold themselves by being exercised, his ideas are so extended, his sentiments so exalted, and his whole mind so enlarged and refined, that if, by abusing his new condition, he did not sometimes degrade it even below that from which he emerged, he ought to bless continually the happy moment that snatched him forever from it, and transformed him from a circumscribed and stupid animal to an intelligent being and a man.

In order to draw a balance between the advantages and disadvantages attending his new situation, let us state them in such a manner that they may be easily compared. Man loses by the social contract his *natural* liberty, and an unlimited right to all which tempts him, and which he can obtain; in return he acquires *civil* liberty, and proprietorship of all he possesses. That we may not be deceived in the value of these compensations, we must distinguish natural liberty, which knows no bounds but the power of the individual, from civil liberty, which is limited by the general will; and between possession, which is only the effect of force or of the right of the first occupant, from property, which must be founded on a positive title. In addition we might add to the other acquisitions of the civil state that of moral liberty, which alone renders a man master of himself; for it is *slavery* to be under the impulse of mere appetite, and *freedom* to obey a law which we prescribe for ourselves. But I have already said too much on this head, and the philosophical sense of the word "liberty" is not at present my subject.

CHAPTER IX

Of Real Property

EACH MEMBER of the community, at the moment of its formation, gives himself up to it just as he is: himself and all his forces, of which his wealth forms a part. By this act, however, possession does not change in nature when it changes its master, and become property when it falls into the hands of the Sovereign; but as the forces of the city are infinitely greater than those of an individual, it is better secured when it becomes a public possession, without being more justifiable, at least with respect to foreigners. As to its members, the State is made master of all their wealth by the social contract, which within the State serves as the basis of all rights; but with regard to other powers, it claims only under the title of first occupancy, which it derives from individuals.

The right of the first occupant, though more substantial than that of the strongest, does not become a real right, until after the right of property is established. All men have naturally a right to whatever is necessary for them; but the act which renders a man the positive proprietor of any property excludes him from everything else. This being accomplished, the possessor must confine himself to what is thus made his own, and he can claim no right beyond it against the community. It is by this means that the right of the first occupant, so weak in the state of nature, is respected by every man in civil society. In this right we respect less what is another's than what is not our own.

The following conditions are in general necessary to give validity to the right founded on first occupancy in any domain whatever. In the first place, the land must not yet be inhabited by any person; secondly, the party must not occupy more land than is sufficient to supply him with subsistence; thirdly, he must take possession, not by a vain ceremony, but by labour and cultivation, as they are the only proofs of a man's being a proprietor, which, in default of a legal title, deserve to be respected by others.

Is not the thus granting the right of first occupancy to *want* and to *labour* extending it as far as it can go? Cannot the right have some bounds assigned to it? Is it sufficient to set our foot on a common domain, and pretend from thence a right to possess it? Is there nothing necessary but sufficient force to drive others out for a moment in order to deprive them of their right of ever returning thither? And how can a man, or a people, overrun an immense territory, and prevent all other human beings from participating in it without being guilty of a criminal usurpation, since they deprive by that means the rest of mankind of a place of residence and of the means of subsistence which nature gave in common to all? When Nuñez Balboa took possession, on the shores of the South Sea, of that ocean and of all South America in the name of the crown of Castille, was that act sufficient to dispossess the inhabitants of the country, and exclude all the princes of the world from settling there? At this rate these ceremonies would have been multiplied extravagantly, and the Catholic king might at one stroke have taken possession of the whole universe without going out of his closet, except indeed to have cut off from his empire what had been previously occupied by other princes.

We see how the lands of private persons, contiguous and united, become the public territory, and how the right of sovereignty, extending from the subjects over the lands they occupy, becomes at once real and personal; by which the occupants are rendered more dependent, and their own force made the guarantee of their fidelity; an advantage which does not seem to have been perceived by ancient monarchs, who, styling themselves Kings of the Persians, the Scythians, or the Macedonians, appear to have regarded themselves as the chiefs of men rather than as masters of the country. Those of the present day call themselves more cleverly Kings of France, Spain, England, etc.; and in thus holding the domain, they are sure to hold its inhabitants.

The singular circumstance attending this alienation is that, in accepting the property of individuals, the community is far from despoiling them, and only ensures them justifiable possession, changes usurpation into a true right, and enjoyment into property. By this means, the possessors being considered as depositaries of the public good, their rights are respected by all the members of the State, and protected with all their force against foreigners. So that by a resignation, advantageous to the public, and still more so to the resigners, they may be justly said to have acquired all that they gave up: a paradox which will be easily explained by distinguishing, as I shall do hereafter, between the rights which the Sovereign and the proprietors have in the same property.

It may also happen that men begin to associate before they have any possessions, and that, spreading afterwards over a country sufficient for them all, they may either enjoy it in common, or part it between them equally, or in such proportions as the Sovereign shall direct. In whatever manner the acquisition is made, the right which each individual has over his own property is always subordinate to the right which the community has over all; without which there would be no solidity in the social bond, nor any real force in the exercise of sovereignty.

I shall conclude this chapter and book with a remark which must serve for the basis of the whole social system: it is that, instead of destroying the natural equality of mankind, the fundamental compact substitutes, on the contrary, a moral and legal equality for that physical inequality which nature placed among men, and that, let men be ever so unequal in strength or in genius, they are all equalized by convention and legal right.[1]

[1] Under bad governments this equality is but an illusive appearance, which only serves to keep the poor in misery, and support the rich in their usurpations. In fact, laws are always useful to those who have abundance, and injurious to those who have nothing: from whence it follows that the social state is only advantaeous to men when every individual has some property, and n o one has too much.

BOOK II

CHAPTER I

That Sovereignty is Inalienable

The first and most important consequence of the principles already established is that the general will alone can direct the forces of the State agreeably to the end of its institution, which is the common good; for if the clashing of private interests has rendered the establishing of societies necessary, the agreement of the same interests has made such establishments possible. It is what is common in these different interests that forms the social bond; and if there was not some point in which they all unanimously centered, no society could exist. It is on the basis of this common interest alone that society must be governed.

I say, therefore, that sovereignty, being only the exercise of the general will, can never alienate itself, and that the Sovereign, which is only a collective being, cannot be represented but by itself: the *power* may well be transmitted but not the *will*.

Indeed, if it is not impossible that a private will should accord on some point with the general will, it is at least impossible that such agreement should be regular and lasting; for the private will is inclined by its nature to partiality, and the general will to impartiality.[1] It is even more impossible to guarantee the continuance of this agreement, even if we were to see it always exist; because that existence must be owing not to art but to chance. The Sovereign may indeed say: "My will at present actually agrees with the will of such and such a man, or at least with what he declares to be his will"; but it cannot say, "Our wills shall likewise agree tomorrow"; since it would be absurd for the will to bind itself for the future, and since it does not belong to any will to consent to what might be injurious to the being from whom the will proceeds. If, therefore, the people promise unconditionally to obey, the act of making such a promise

[1] [*La volonté particulière tend, par sa nature, aux préférences, et la volonté générale à l'égalité.*]

23

People cannot promise continually To agree

dissolves their existence, and they lose their quality of a people; for at the moment that there is a master, there is no longer a Sovereign, and from that moment the body politic is destroyed.[2]

I do not say that the commands of chiefs cannot pass for general wills, so long as the Sovereign, being free to oppose them, does not do so. In such cases we must presume from their silence that the people yield their consent. But I shall explain this more at large presently.

Passive consent

CHAPTER II

That Sovereignty is Indivisible

FOR THE SAME REASON that sovereignty is inalienable, it is indivisible. For the will is general[1] or it is not; it is either the will of the whole body of the people, or only of a part. In the first case, this declared will is an act of sovereignty and constitutes law; in the second, it is but a private will or an act of magistracy, and is at most but a decree.

But our political thinkers, not being able to divide sovereignty in principle, have divided it in its object: into force and will; legislative power and executive power; the rights of levying taxes, of administering justice, and making war; the internal government and the power of treating with foreigners. But by sometimes confounding all these parts, and sometimes separating them, they make of the sovereign power a fantastical being composed of related pieces; as if man were composed of several bodies, one with eyes, another with arms, another with feet, but none with anything more. The mountebanks of Japan are said to dismember an infant in the sight of the spectators, throw its limbs one after another into the air, and make the child come down alive and whole. The tricks of our political jugglers are very similar,

[2] [Compare the opposing views of Hobbes (in *Leviathan*) and of Grotius (especially *The Law of War and Peace*, Bk. II, chap. 4), against whom these arguments are directed.]

[1] To make the will general, it is not always necessary that it should be unanimous; but it is indispensably necessary that every vote should be counted: any formal exclusion destroys generality.

for after dismembering the social body by a sleight worthy of the black art, they bring its parts together again, nobody knows how.

This error arises from our not having formed exact ideas of the sovereign authority, and from our taking for parts of that authority what are only its emanations. For example, the acts of declaring war and making peace are considered as acts of sovereignty, when in fact they are not so, because neither of these acts is a law, but only the application of the law, a particular act which determines the application of the law, as we shall clearly perceive when the idea attached to the word "law" is fixed.

By tracing in the same manner the other divisions, we should find that whenever we suppose sovereignty divided we deceive ourselves; that the rights which we take for a part of that sovereignty are all subordinate to it, and always suppose supreme wills of which they only sanction the execution.

It is impossible to express how greatly this want of exactness has obscured the arguments and conclusions of writers on political right, when they have attempted to decide on the respective rights of kings and peoples by the principles which they have themselves laid down. Every person may see in the third and fourth chapters of the First Book of Grotius,[2] how that learned man and his translator, Barbeyrac, have entangled and embarrassed themselves in their sophisms, fearful of saying too much, or of not saying enough to answer their designs, and apprehensive of clashing with those interests which they had to conciliate.

Grotius, discontented with his own country, took refuge in France; and endeavouring to make his court to Louis XIII, to whom his book is dedicated, he has spared no pains to despoil the people of all their rights and transfer them to their kings in the most artful manner. This was also the design of Barbeyrac, who dedicated his translation to George I, King of England. But unfortunately the expulsion of James II, which he calls "abdication," obliged him to proceed very cautiously, to shuffle and evade, that he might avoid making King William appear a usurper. If these two writers had adopted the true principles, all their difficulties would have been removed, and they would have been always consistent; but the task of speaking truth, and recommending themselves to no favour but that of the people,

[2] [*Op. cit.*]

would have been to them a vexatious one. Truth does not lead to fortune, and the people have neither ambassadorships, professorships, nor pensions to bestow.

CHAPTER III

WHETHER THE GENERAL WILL CAN ERR

IT FOLLOWS from what has been said that the general will is always right and tends always to the public advantage; but it does not follow that the deliberations of the people have always the same rectitude. Our will always seeks our own good, but we do not always perceive what it is. The people are never corrupted, but they are often deceived, and only then do they seem to will what is bad.

There is frequently much difference between the *will of all* and the *general will*. The latter regards only the common interest; the former regards private interest, and is indeed but a sum of private wills:[1] but remove from these same wills the pluses and minuses that cancel each other, and then the general will remains as the sum of the differences.[2]

If, when the people, sufficiently informed, deliberated, there was to be no communication among them, from the grand total of trifling differences the general will would always result, and their resolutions be always good. But when cabals and partial associations are formed at the expense of the great association, the will of each such association, though *general* with regard to its members, is *private* with regard to the State: it can then be said no longer that there are as many voters as men, but only as many as there are associations. By this means the differences being less numerous, they produce a result less general. Finally, when one of these associations becomes so large

---

[1] [*volontés particulières.*]

[2] "Each interest," says the Marquis d'A. [d'Argenson], "has its different principles. The agreement of two private interests is formed by opposition to a third." He might have added that the agreement of all interests is produced by opposition to that of each. If there were no different interests, we should scarcely perceive the common interest, which never finds any opposer; everything would go on regularly of itself, and politics be no longer an art.

that it prevails over all the rest, you have no longer the sum of many opinions dissenting in a small degree from each other, but one great dictating dissentient; from that moment there is no longer a general will, and the predominating opinion is only an individual one.

It is therefore of the utmost importance for obtaining the expression of the general will, that no partial society should be formed in the State, and that every citizen should speak his opinion entirely from himself:[1] such was the unique and sublime system of the great Lycurgus. When there are partial societies, it is politic to multiply their number, that they may be all kept on an equality. This method was pursued by Solon, Numa, and Servius. These are the only precautions that can be taken to make the general will always intelligent, and prevent the people from being deceived.

CHAPTER IV

OF THE LIMITS OF THE SOVEREIGN POWER

IF THE STATE or city is only a moral person, the existence of which consists in the union of its members, and if its most important care is that of preserving itself, there is a necessity for its possessing a universally compulsive power, for moving and disposing each part in the manner most convenient to the whole. As nature gives to every man absolute command over all his members, the social compact gives to the body politic absolute command over the members of which it is formed; and it is this power, when directed by the general will, that bears, as I have said before, the name of "sovereignty."

But, besides the public person, we have to consider the private persons who compose it, and whose lives and liberty are naturally independent of it. The point here is to distinguish properly between

---

[1] "Divisions" says Machiavelli, "sometimes injure and sometimes serve a republic. The injury is done by cabals and factions, the service by a party which maintains itself without cabals or faction. Since, therefore, it is impossible for the founder of a republic to provide against enmities, he must make the best provision he can against factions." (*History of Florence*, Bk. VII.) [Rousseau retains the quotation in the original Italian.]

the respective rights of the citizens and the Sovereign,[1] and between the duties which the former have to fulfil in quality of subjects, and the natural rights which they ought to enjoy in quality of men.

It is granted that all which an individual alienates by the social compact is only that part of his power, his property, and his liberty, the use of which is important to the community; but we must also grant that the Sovereign is the only judge of what is important to the community.

All the services which a citizen can render to the State ought to be rendered as soon as the Sovereign demands them; but the Sovereign cannot, on its side, impose any burden on the subject useless to the community; it cannot even have the inclination to do so; for, under the law of reason, nothing is done without a cause, any more than under the law of nature.

The engagements which bind us to the social body are only obligatory because they are mutual; and their nature is such that in fulfilling them we cannot labour for others without labouring at the same time for ourselves. Wherefore is the general will always right, and wherefore do all the wills invariably seek the happiness of every individual among them, if it is not that there is no person who does not appropriate the word "each" to himself, and who does not think of himself when he is voting for all? This proves that the equality of right, and the idea of justice which it inspires, is derived from the preference which each gives to himself, and consequently from the nature of man; that the general will, to be truly such, ought to be so in its object, as well as its essence: that it ought to come from all, if we are to apply it to all; and that it loses its natural rectitude when it tends towards any one individual and determinate object, because then, judging of what is external to us, we have no true principle of equity to guide us.

In fact, as soon as it is a matter of an individual fact or right, on any point which has not been previously regulated by a general convention, the affair becomes contentious. It is a process wherein the persons interested are one of the parties, and the public the other, but where I do not see any law that must be followed, or any judge

---

[1] Attentive readers, be not too hasty, I beg of you, to accuse me of contradicting myself. I could not avoid doing so terminologically, on account of the poverty of the language; but have patience until I explain my meaning.

who ought to decide. It would be ridiculous in such a case to bring the question to an express decision of the general will, which could only be the conclusion of one party, and consequently, which would be, with respect to the other party, but an external and private will, hurried on that occasion into injustice, and subject to error. Thus, in the same manner as a private will cannot represent the general will, the general will, in its turn, changes its nature if its object is private,[2] and cannot, as the general will, pronounce either on a man or a fact. When the people of Athens, for example, nominated or cashiered their chiefs, decreed honours to one, imposed punishments on another, and, by the multitude of their private decrees, exercised indiscriminately all the acts of government, the people, properly speaking, had then no longer a general will; they acted no longer as Sovereign but as magistrate. This will appear contradictory to common ideas; but I must have time to unfold mine.

We should perceive by this that the generality of the will depends less on the number of voters than on the common interest which unites them; for, in this institution, each necessarily submits to the conditions which he imposes on others — an admirable union of interest and justice, which gives to the common deliberations a character of equity that vanishes in the discussion of all private affairs for want of a common interest to combine and identify the ruling of the judge with that of the party.

By whatever path we return to our principle, we always arrive at the same conclusion — that is, that the social compact establishes among citizens such an equality that they are all engaged under the same conditions, and should all enjoy the same rights. Thus, by the nature of the compact all acts of sovereignty, that is to say, all authentic acts of the general will, oblige or favour all citizens alike in such a manner as evinces that the Sovereign knows no person but the body of the nation, and does not make any distinction among the individuals who compose it. What, therefore, is properly an act of sovereignty? It is not a convention between a superior and an inferior, but a convention of the body with each of its members — a justifiable convention because it has the social contract for its basis; equitable, because it is common to all; beneficial, because it can have no other object but the general good; and solid, because it is guaranteed by the

[2] [un objet particulier.]

public force and the supreme power. While subjects are under the governance of such conventions only, they obey no one but only their own will: and to enquire how far the respective rights of the Sovereign and citizens extend is to ask how far the citizens can engage with themselves, each towards all, and all towards each.

We see by this that the sovereign power, all absolute, all sacred, all inviolable as it is, neither will, nor can, exceed the bounds of general conventions, and that every man may fully dispose of what is left to him of his property and his liberty by these conventions; so that the Sovereign never has any right to lay a greater charge on one subject than on another, because then the affair would become personal,[1] and in such cases the power of the Sovereign is no longer competent.

These distinctions once admitted, it is evidently false that individuals have made any real renunciation by the social contract. On the contrary, they find their situation, by the effect of that contract, really rendered preferable to what it was before. Instead of making any alienation they have only made an advantageous transition from a mode of living unsettled and precarious to one better and more secure, from a state of natural independence to one of liberty, from possessing the power of injuring others to security for themselves, and from their strength, which others might, by the employment of theirs, overcome, to a right which social union renders invincible. Even their lives, which they have devoted to the State, are continually protected by it; and when they are exposed in its defence, what is it but restoring that which they have received from it? What do they do but what they would do more frequently, and with more danger, in the state of nature, when, living in continual and unavoidable conflicts, they would have to defend at the peril of their lives what was necessary to the preservation of life? All, it is true, must fight for their country when their service is requisite; but then no person has occasion to fight for himself as an individual. And is it not gaining a great advantage to be obliged, for the protection of that to which we owe our security, to incur occasionally only a part of that danger to which we must be again exposed as individuals as soon as we were deprived of it?

[1] [l'affaire devenant particulière.]

CHAPTER V

OF THE RIGHT OF LIFE AND DEATH

IT MAY BE ASKED how individuals, having no right to dispose of their own lives, can transmit to the Sovereign a right which they do not possess. This question appears difficult to solve only because it is improperly stated. Every man has a right to risk his own life for the preservation of it. Was any man ever said to intend suicide when he throws himself from a window to avoid the flames? Is that crime imputed to him who perishes at sea in a tempest because, at the time of his embarkation, he knew of the danger?

The end of the social treaty is the preservation of the contracting parties. Whoever wants to enjoy the end must will the means, and some risks, and even some dangers, are inseparable from these means. The man who would preserve his life at the expense of the lives of others ought in turn to expose his own for their protection when it is necessary. The citizen is not a judge of the peril to which the law may expose him; and when the prince[1] says to him, "It is expedient for the State that thou shouldst die," he ought to die, because it is only on that condition that he has enjoyed his security up to that moment, and because his life is not to be considered simply as the boon of nature, but as a conditional gift from the State.

The punishment of death inflicted on criminals may be considered from the same point of view: it is to secure himself from being the victim of assassins that a man consents to die if he becomes an assassin. In this treaty the parties are so far from disposing of their own lives that they think only of guarding them, and it is not to be supposed that, at the time of contracting, any of the contracting parties intends to deserve the gallows.

Further, every malefactor, by attacking the social right, becomes by his crimes a rebel and a traitor to his country; by violating its laws, he ceases to be a member of it and, in fact, makes war upon it. The existence of the State then becomes incompatible with his; one of the two must therefore perish; and when the criminal is executed he suffers less as a citizen than as an enemy. The proceedings against him, and the judgment pronounced in consequence, are the proofs and the

[1] [i.e., the government — *cf.* p. 51.]

declaration that he has broken the social treaty, and, consequently, that he is no longer a member of the State. But, as he is still considered as such at least while he sojourns there, he must be either removed by exile, as a violator of the pact, or by death, as a public enemy; for such an enemy is not a moral person, he is simply a man: and it is then that it is the right of war to kill the vanquished.

But, it may be asked, is not the condemnation of a criminal an individual act? I grant it: but this condemnation of a criminal does not pertain to the Sovereign; it is a right which the Sovereign can confer, though it cannot itself exercise it. My ideas are consistent, but I cannot explain them all at one time.

It might be added that the frequency of punishments is always a sign of a weak or indolent government. There is no one so vile that he may not be rendered good for something. There is no right to put any one to death, even as an example, except the man whose life cannot be preserved without danger to the State.

In regard to the right of pardon, or exempting a criminal from the sentence directed by the law and pronounced against him by the judge, it pertains only to that which is above the law and the judge, that is, to the Sovereign; but its right in this case is not very clear, and occasions for using it occur but seldom. In a well-governed State there are few punishments, not because there are many pardons, but because there are only a small number of criminals. When the State is declining, the multitude of crimes assures impunity. Under the Roman Republic neither the senate nor the consuls ever attempted to pardon any criminal; nor did even the people, though they sometimes revoked their own sentence. The frequency of pardons announces that crime will soon have no need for them, and it is easy to see what that must lead to. But my heart murmurs and restrains my pen: let us leave the discussion of these questions to the just man who has never erred, nor had himself need for pardon.

CHAPTER VI

OF THE LAW

BY THE SOCIAL COMPACT we have given existence and life to the body politic; it now remains to give it motion and will by legislation. For the original act by which the body is formed and united determines none of the measures that ought to be taken for its preservation.

What is good, and conformable to order, is so from the nature of things, and independently of human conventions. All justice flows from God, he alone is the source of it; and if we knew how to receive it from on high, we should require neither government nor laws. This justice is undoubtedly universal and emanates from reason alone; but this justice, to be admitted among us, must be reciprocal. Humanly speaking, the laws of justice, when they have no natural sanction, are vain among men; they are only injurious to the just and advantageous to the wicked part of mankind, for the just man invariably adheres to its rules with respect to everyone, but no one adheres to them towards him. There must therefore be conventions and laws to combine our duties and our rights, and to direct justice to its end. In the state of nature, where everything is in common, I owe nothing to those to whom I have promised nothing; and I do not acknowledge that anything, but what I do not wish to use, can be the property of another person. It is not so in the civil order, where every right is determined by law.

But what, in fine, is a law? While men content themselves with affixing none but metaphysical ideas to this word, they must continue to reason without understanding one another; and when they have said what a law of nature is, they will still be no less ignorant of what a law of the State is.

I have already said that there can be no general will directed towards a private object. That private object is either in the State, or outside the State. If it is outside the State, a will which is alien to it cannot be general with regard to it; and if it is in the State, it makes a part of it, and between the whole and its part there is a relation which proves the existence of two separate beings; of which the said part makes one, and the whole — less that same part — makes the other. But the whole less a part is not the whole; and while this relation subsists, there is no whole, but two unequal parts: from whence it follows that the will of one part cannot in any way be general with respect to the other.

But when the whole people determines for the whole people, it considers only itself; and if a relation is then formed it is only a relation of the whole object from one point of view to the whole object from another point of view, and the whole itself is not divided. Then the affair on which they enact is general, as is the will that enacts. It is this act that I call a "law."

When I say that the object of the laws is always general, I mean that the law views its subjects collectively and their actions abstractly, never a man as individual or an action as private. Thus the law may enact that there shall be certain privileges, but it cannot name the persons who are to enjoy them; the law may divide the citizens into several classes, and specify the qualifications which shall give a right of admission to each class; but it cannot direct such or such a person to be admitted; the law can establish a monarchical government and an hereditary succession, but it cannot elect a king or name a royal family. In a word, all those functions which relate to any individual object pertain not to the legislative power.

Under this idea, we perceive at once how unnecessary it would be to enquire to whom the function of making laws belongs, because the laws are but the acts of the general will; neither need we ask whether the prince is above the laws, since he is a member of the State; nor whether the law can be unjust, as no one is unjust towards himself; nor how we can be free while subjected to the laws, since they are but the registers of our own wills.

We see also that, since the law unites universality of will with universality of object, whatever is ordered of his own accord by any man, whoever he may be, is not law; nay, even that which the Sovereign orders relative to a private object is not a law but a decree; neither is it an act of sovereignty but of magistracy.

I therefore denominate every State a "republic" which is governed by laws, under whatever form of administration it may be; for then only the public interest governs, and the affairs of the public obtain a due regard.[1] All justifiable governments are republican;[2] and I will hereafter explain what government is.

The laws are properly but the conditions of civil association. The people submit themselves to the laws, and ought to enjoy the right of making them; it pertains only to those who associate to regulate

[1] [*Car alors seulement. . . la chose publique est quelque chose.*]

[2] I do not by the word "republic" mean an aristocracy or democracy only, but in general all governments guided by the general will, which is the law. To be justifiable, the government should not be confounded with the Sovereign, but be considered as its administrator. Then monarchy itself would be a republic. This will be further explained in the following book.

the terms of the society. But how do they regulate them? Is it by
a common agreement, by a sudden inspiration? Has the body politic
an organ for declaring its will? Who gives to that body the necessary
foresight to form these acts and publish them beforehand? Or how
are they declared at the moment of need? How can an unenlightened
multitude, which often does not know what it wants, since it so seldom
knows what is good for it, execute, of itself, so great, so difficult an
enterprise as a system of legislation? Of themselves the people always
will the good, but of themselves they do not always see in what it
consists. The general will is always right, but the judgment that
guides it is not always enlightened. It is therefore necessary to make
the people see things as they are, and sometimes as they ought to
appear, to point out to them the right path which they are seeking,
to guard them from the seducing voice of private wills, and, helping
them to see how times and places are connected, to induce them to
balance the attraction of immediate and sensible advantage against
the apprehension of unknown and distant evil. Individuals see the
good they reject; the public wills the good it does not see. All have
equally need for guidance. Some must have their wills made conformable to their reason, and others must be taught what it is they will.
From this increase of public knowledge would result the union of
judgment and will in the social body; from that union comes the
harmony of the parties and the highest power of the whole. From
thence is born the necessity of a legislator.

CHAPTER VII

OF THE LEGISLATOR

TO DISCOVER those happy rules of government which would agree
with every nation could only be the work of some superior intelligence,
acquainted with all the passions of men, but liable to none of them;
who, without bearing any affinity to our nature, knew it perfectly;
whose happiness was independent of ours, but who still condescended
to make us the object of his care; and who having persevered through
a long course of years in the pursuit of distant glory, could enjoy

in other ages the reward of his unwearied zeal.[1] In short, gods would be required to give laws to mankind.

The same reasoning which Caligula used with respect to fact Plato employed with respect to right in order to define the civil man or prince in his dialogue, *The Statesman*. But if it be true that a great prince is a rare man, how much more rare must be a good legislator? The first has only to follow the model which the other has to form. One is the scientific mechanician, who invents the machine, the other is the mere mechanic, who winds it up and sets it in motion. "At the birth of societies," says Montesquieu, "the chiefs of the republics form the institutions, but afterwards the institutions form the chiefs."[2]

Those who dare to undertake the institution of a people must feel themselves capable, as it were, of changing human nature, of transforming each individual, who by himself is a perfect and solitary whole, into a part of a much greater whole, from which he in some measure receives his being and his life; of altering the constitution of man for the purpose of strengthening it; of substituting a moral and partial existence instead of the physical and independent existence which we have all received from nature. They must, in a word, remove from man his own proper energies to bestow upon him those which are strange to him, and which he cannot employ without the assistance of others. The more those natural powers are annihilated, the more august and permanent are those which he acquires, and the more solid and perfect is the institution: so that if each citizen is nothing and can do nothing but when combined with all the other citizens, and the force acquired by the whole from this combination is equal or superior to the sum of all the natural forces of all these individuals, it may be said that legislation is at the highest point of perfection which human talents can attain.

The legislator is in every sense a most extraordinary man in the State. If he must be so from his genius, he is no less so from his employment, which is neither magistracy nor sovereignty. This

[1] A people do not become celebrated until their legislation begins to decline. We do not know during how many ages the Lacedemonians lived happily under the laws of Lycurgus before there was any account made of them by the rest of Greece.

[2] [*Grandeur et décadence des Romains*, Chap. I. — Montesquieu (1689-1755) is best known for his extremely influential *L'esprit des lois* ("The Spirit of the Laws"), which was published in 1748.]

employment, which constitutes the republic, enters not into its constitution; it is a particular and superior function, which has nothing in common with human empire; because, if he who commands men must not preside over the laws, he who presides over the laws must not have the command over men: otherwise his laws, employed as the ministers of his passions, would frequently merely perpetuate his injustices; and it would be impossible to prevent private aims from defiling the sanctity of his work.

When Lycurgus gave laws to his country, he began by abdicating the royal power. It was the custom with most of the cities of Greece to confide the establishment of their legislation to strangers. The modern republics of Italy have imitated their example; Geneva also did so, and found it to its advantage.[3] Rome in her most glorious days saw all the crimes of tyranny revive within her bosom, and herself on the very eve of perishing, by having united in the same men the legislative authority and the sovereign power.

But even the decemvirs themselves never arrogated the right of making any law by their own authority alone. "Nothing which we propose to you," said they to the people, "can pass into law without your consent. Romans, be you yourselves the authors of the laws which must ensure your happiness."

He who compiles the laws, therefore, has not, nor ought he to have, any right to legislate, and the people cannot, even if they should be inclined, deprive themselves of that incommunicable right, because, according to the fundamental compact, it is only the general will that can compel individuals, and it can never be known whether a private will is conformable to the general will until it has been submitted to the free vote of the people. I have affirmed this already, but a repetition may not be useless.

Thus we find at the same time in the work of legislation two things which seem incompatible with each other: an enterprise exceeding human power, executed by an authority which is not an authority.

[3] Those who consider Calvin only as a theologian are little acquainted with the extent of his genius. The compilation of our wise edicts, in which he had so large a part, does him as much honour as his *Institute*. Whatever revolution time may bring about in our religion, while patriotism and the love of liberty are not wholly extinct among us, the memory of that great man will never cease to have the benediction of the Genevans.

There is also another difficulty which deserves attention. Sages who wish to use their own language in addressing the vulgar instead of vulgar language cannot possibly make themselves understood. For after all, there are a multitude of ideas which it is impossible to express in the language of the people. Views that are too general, and objects that are too remote, are equally beyond their comprehension; and every individual, relishing no scheme of government but that which promotes his own private interest, cannot easily be made sensible of the benefits to be derived from the continual privations imposed upon him by wholesome laws. For a new-born people to relish wise maxims of policy and to pursue the fundamental rules of statecraft, it would be necessary that the effect should become the cause; that the social mind, which should be the product of such institution, should prevail even at the institution of society; and that men should be, before the formation of laws, what those laws alone can make them. The legislator being, from these reasons, unable to employ either force or argument, he must have recourse to an authority of another order, which can bear men away without violence, and persuade without convincing them.

It is this that has, in all ages, obliged the founders of nations to have recourse to the intervention of Heaven and to attribute to the gods what has proceeded from their own wisdom, that the people might submit to the laws of the State as to those of nature and, recognizing that the same power which formed man created the city, obey freely, and contentedly endure that restraint so necessary to the public happiness.

This sublime reason, so far above the comprehension of vulgar men, is that whose decisions legislators put in the mouth of the immortals, that those might be led along under the sanction of divine authority, whom it might be impossible for human prudence to conduct without it.[4] But it belongs not to all men to make the gods speak, nor to gain belief if they pretend to be the interpreters of the divine will. The

---

[4] "It is true," says Machiavelli, "there never was, in any country, a promulgator of extraordinary laws who had not recourse to God; because otherwise his system would not have been received; a wise man may know many useful truths, though they are not so self-evident as to carry conviction to the minds of others." (*Discourses on Livy*, Bk. V, chap. 11). [Rousseau retains the quotation in the original Italian.]

magnanimous spirit of the legislator is the sole miracle which must
prove his mission. Any man may engrave upon tables of stone,
purchase an oracle, pretend a secret intercourse with some divinity,
teach a bird to whisper in his ear, or find some other means as gross
as these to impose upon the people. But whoever depends entirely
on such arts, though he may chance to draw a crowd of superstitious
fools around him, can never lay the foundation of an empire, and his
extravagant undertaking will soon perish with himself. Illusions can
form but transitory bonds; it is wisdom alone that renders them
permanent. The Jewish law, which still subsists, and that of the
child of Ishmæl, which, for ten centuries, has governed half the
world, still proclaim the great men by whom they were dictated; and
while the pride of philosophy and the blindness of party prejudice
will see in these men only fortunate impostures, the true political
thinker admires in their institutions that great and comprehensive
genius which presides over durable establishments.

After this I should not conclude, with Warburton, that politics and
religion have with us one common object, but that, in the origin
of nations, the one serves as the instrument of the other.[1]

CHAPTER VIII

OF THE PEOPLE

AS AN ARCHITECT, before he begins to erect a large edifice, examines
whether the ground is strong enough to support the weight, so the
wise lawgiver does not begin by drawing up laws which are good in
themselves, but considers whether the people they are designed to
govern are likely to carry them into effect. After such an examination,
Plato refused to legislate for the Arcadians and Cyreneans, well
knowing that, as these two peoples were wealthy, they could never
submit to equality; Minos, though the Cretans were a vicious people,
attempted to discipline them; but under excellent laws the people of
Crete continued vile.

[1] [William Warburton (1698–1779) was a vigorous anti-deist writer, who became
bishop of Gloucester in 1759.]

A thousand nations have made a brilliant appearance on earth who could never have submitted to the governance of good laws; and even those who could have submitted to good laws could have done so for only a very transitory period in their long history. Most peoples, like most human beings, are docile only in their youth, and become more stubborn as their age advances. When once customs are established, and prejudices have taken root, it is idle and dangerous to attempt their reformation; the people, like cowardly and stupid patients who tremble at the sight of their physician, will not even bear to have their evils examined into with a view to removing them.

But just as there are certain diseases incident to men, which derange the reason, and efface all remembrance of the past, so we sometimes find in the history of States that a violent epoch or a revolution has such influence on the minds of the people that the horror which attends the recollection of what has happened produces the same effect as forgetfulness does in the individual; and the State, after being set in flames by civil wars, is born again, as it were, from her own ashes, and recovers all the vigour of youth as it leaves the arms of death. Such was Sparta in the time of Lycurgus, such was Rome after the Tarquins, and, in our time, such have been Holland and Switzerland after the expulsion of the tyrants.

But these events are rare; they are exceptions, the cause of which can only arise from the particular constitution of the State concerned. They can never even happen twice to the same people; because, though men may become free as long as they are still in a state of barbarism, they cannot do so again after civil energy is exhausted. Then troubles may destroy it, but revolutions can never re-establish it; and when the chains of such a people are once broken, it falls asunder, and exists no more: henceforth they need a master, and not a liberator. Oh ye peoples who are free, remember this maxim: "Liberty may be acquired, but never recovered."

Youth is not infancy. There is with nations as with men a period of youth, or, shall I say, maturity, which it is proper they should attain before they are made subject to laws: but it is not always easy to know when a people are sufficiently matured; and, if the moment is anticipated, the work is defeated. One people can be disciplined at birth, another not at the end of ten centuries. The Russians will never be perfectly civilized, because their civilization was attempted too hastily. Peter had a genius for imitation, but he did not possess those great talents which can create and establish everything from nothing. Some of his measures were good, but most of them were ill-timed. He saw that his people were barbarous, but he did not see that they were unripe for civilization; he wanted to civilize them when they needed only to be inured to hardships. Peter was desirous of making them Germans or English, when he should first have made them Russians. By this unwise proceeding, he has forever prevented his subjects from becoming what they might have been, by persuading them that they were what they were not. It is just in the same manner that a French preceptor forms his pupil, so that he shines while in his childish days, and then becomes a nonentity. The Russian empire will want to subjugate all Europe, and will be subjugated herself. The Tartars, now its dependents and neighbours, will soon become its masters, and also ours: this revolution seems to me to be inevitable. All the European princes seem labouring in concert to accelerate the event.

CHAPTER IX

OF THE PEOPLE — *Continued*

As NATURE has determined the size of a well-constructed man, beyond which nature makes only giants or dwarfs, so there are certain limitations for the constitution of a State, to which, if it does not adhere, it ceases to be at its best. If it be too large, it cannot be properly governed; if too small, it cannot support itself. There is in all bodies politic a certain *maximum* of force which they cannot exceed, and which they only lose by their aggrandizement. The social bond is enfeebled by extension; and in general a small State is proportionally stronger than a great one.

There are a thousand reasons to support this maxim. First, administration becomes more difficult in proportion as the place where it is exercised is removed from the centre of government, just as a weight becomes heavier at the extremity of a longer lever. Administration therefore becomes more oppressive in proportion to its increasing distance; for, in the first place, every corporate town has its own administrative bodies, which the people must pay for; every district has its own, which the people still must pay for; then comes every province, then the great governments, the satrapies and vice-royalties, each supported still more extravagantly than the other, as it rises above it in degree, and all at the charge of the unhappy people; last of these comes the supreme administration, which crushes down all with its weight. The subjects are exhausted by the enormity of all these expenses: they are so far from being better governed by these different orders of administrators that they would be happier under the direction of one single chief. When the affairs of a State are in this situation, there are scarcely resources for use in case of an emergency; and if these are required, the State finds itself upon the eve of ruin.

This is not all; not only does the government have less vigour and activity to enforce the observance of the laws, prevent vexations, correct abuses, and keep the spirit of sedition from being kindled in distant places, but the people have less affection for the chiefs they never see, and for their country, which seems like the world to them, and for their fellow countrymen, with the greater part of whom they have no acquaintance. The same laws will not suit so many diverse provinces which have different manners, are situated in the most different climates, and which will never submit to the same form of government. Different laws serve only to create trouble and confusion among peoples who, living under the same chiefs and having continual intercourse with one another, pass to and fro and intermarry, and, submitting to different customs, often cannot know if they can call their very patrimony their own. Talents are overlooked, virtue remains unknown, and vice is suffered to escape with impunity among this multitude of men unknown to one another, whom the central administration has gathered together in one place. The chiefs, fatigued by a multiplicity of affairs, see nothing for themselves; and clerks govern the State. Finally, the measures which it is necessary to pursue for maintaining the general authority, which all these distant officials want to escape or to impose upon, absorb the public care; there is none left for the welfare of the people, and even for the defense of the State when there is need; and thus a body, too large for its constitution, is pressed down, and perishes under its own weight.

On the other side, it is necessary that the State should have a sufficient basis to give it solidity, to resist the attacks it must inevitably meet with, and to support the exertions necessary to its preservation: because every people has a kind of centrifugal force by which they act continually on each other, and tends to aggrandize itself at the expense of its neighbours, like the vortices of Descartes. Thus the weak would soon be swallowed up; and none could be secure without establishing a general balance of power to make the compressure everywhere nearly equal.

It appears from these observations that there are reasons for extending, and reasons for confining, the limits of the State; and the statesman must possess superior talents who can find, between the two extremes, that golden mean on the adoption of which depends in a great measure the permanency of the State. It can be said, in general, that reasons for expansion are only external and relative, and ought to be subordinated to the reason for contraction, which are internal and absolute. The great point is to establish a sound and strong constitution; and chief dependence must be placed on the vigour generated by a good government rather than on the resources afforded by enlarged dominions.

There have, however, been States so formed that conquests were rendered necessary by the very principles of their constitution, and on a continual increase of empire depended their very being. Perhaps they felicitated themselves on this happy necessity, though it showed them, not only the limits of their greatness, but the inevitable moment of their fall.

CHAPTER X

OF THE PEOPLE — *Continued*

THE BODY POLITIC may be measured in two different ways: by the extent of its territory, and by the number of its people; and there must be a right proportion between both to give true greatness to the State. The men form the State, and the land must sustain the men; therefore, the due proportion is that the land should be sufficient to maintain the inhabitants, and the inhabitants as numerous as the land can support. It is in this right proportion that there is found the *maximum* of force of a given number of people; for, if there be too large a domain, the protection of it is troublesome, the cultivation insufficient, the produce superfluous, and it is in time the cause of involving the State in a defensive war. If the portion of land is too small, the State must depend on the favour of its neighbours for the additional provision it requires; and this proves in time the cause of an offensive war. Every people which has, from its peculiar circumstances, no alternative but war or commerce, is weak in itself. It depends upon its neighbours, it depends on events; it can have but a precarious and short existence. It must change its situation by conquest, or be conquered and become nothing itself. It cannot keep itself free but by being insignificant or by being great.

It is impossible to calculate the exact extent of land and the number of inhabitants that are sufficient for each other, as this must vary according to the qualities and fertility of the soil, the nature of its productions, the influence of climate, and in no small degree on the constitutions and habits of those to be sustained; for some men can subsist on a little in a fertile country, while others will consume a great deal in the most sterile one. We must also pay regard to the degree of fruitfulness of the women, to those local circumstances that may be more or less favourable to population, and to the number of persons whom the legislator can hope to attract to his country by his establishments. In considering these particulars, the legislator must form his judgment from what he foresees rather than from what offers itself immediately to his view, and must not stop at the present state of population, but must make allowance for that increase of people which must naturally be expected. There are, besides, a thousand accidents occurring from local situations that may require, or at least warrant, the acquisition of more land than at first appears necessary. Thus, people are observed to increase much in mountainous countries, where the natural productions, such as woods and pasture, require little labour, where, as experience teaches us, the women are always more fruitful than in the plains, and where a great extent of sloping land affords a comparatively small horizontal base which alone can be counted on for vegetation. On the other hand, when a State establishes itself on the borders of the ocean, even amidst barren rocks and sands, the people can occupy a narrower circle, because there the fish which the sea affords will supply, in a great measure, the deficiency of land productions, because there it is necessary for men to keep more together in order to repel pirates, and because they can from thence more easily send colonies to people other parts of the earth when their inhabitants become too numerous to be maintained at home.

To these conditions for establishing a people we must add one more which cannot take the place of anything else, but without which all the others will be of no effect: the enjoyment of peace and abundance; for the time of forming a State is, like that of forming a battalion of soldiers, the very moment when the body is weakest and most easily destroyed. Men make a more powerful resistance in a state of absolute disorder than at the busy crisis of a new arrangement, when the attention of each person is engaged by his own position and not by the general danger. If either war, famine, or sedition assail them at such time of crisis, the State is inevitably overturned.

I admit that many governments have been established amidst such tempestuous scenes; but they are the very governments that destroy the State. Usurpers frequently kindle or take advantage of these troublesome times in order to establish, by favour of the public terror, such destructive laws as would never be adopted in moments of calmer reason. The choice of the time for instituting any law is one of the surest criteria whether it be the work of a legislator or a tyrant.

What people, then, are in a proper state to receive laws? Those who are already united by some original bond of origin, interest, or convention, but who have not yet had any established system of laws; those in whom neither customs nor superstitions have taken root; those who are not afraid of being borne down by sudden invasion, but who, without entering into the quarrels of their neighbours, can by themselves resist each of them, or be assisted by the one to subdue the other; those whose members may be all known to each other, and among whom there is no necessity for laying a heavier burden on a man than he is able to bear; those who may do without other peoples, and whom other peoples do without;[1] those who are neither rich nor

---

[1] When of two neighbouring peoples the one cannot do without the other, the first is in a very hard situation, and the other in a very dangerous one. All wise nations

poor, but have enough to support themselves; and, finally, those who unite the stability of an established state with the docility of a new people. The arduous work of legislation is made difficult less by what it is necessary to establish than by what it is necessary to destroy; and what makes legislators succeed to seldom is the impossibility of finding the simplicity of nature united with those establishments which are necessary for society. But as we very rarely see all the requisite circumstances combine together, so we seldom find any State well constructed.

There is still in Europe one country capable of receiving legislation: it is the island of Corsica. The valour and constancy with which that brave people have recovered and defended their liberty well deserves to have some wise man step forward and teach them how to preserve it. I have a presentiment that this little island will some day astonish Europe.

CHAPTER XI

Of the Different Systems of Legislation

If we examine in what precisely consists the supreme good of all, which ought to be the object of every system of legislation, it will appear to reduce to two principal points: *liberty* and *equality*; in liberty, because all private dependence[1] subtracts so much force from the body of the State; in equality, because liberty cannot subsist without it.

I have already explained the nature of civil liberty: and, with respect to equality, the word must not be understood to mean that power and riches should be equally divided between all; but that power should never be so strong as to be capable of acts of violence, or

so circumstanced have set their neighbours free from their dependence as soon as possible. The republic of Thlascala, thus shut up within the Mexican empire, chose rather to do without salt than to buy it from the Mexicans, or even to accept it as a gift. The wise Thlascalans saw the secret design of such liberality. They preserved their freedom; and this little State, confined within a great empire, was at length the means of its destruction.

[1] [*dépendence particulière.*]

exercised but in virtue of the exerciser's station, and under the direction of the laws; and that, in regard to riches, no citizen should be sufficiently opulent to be able to purchase another, and none so poor as to be forced to sell himself.[2] This supposes on the side of the great, moderation in wealth and position, and, on the side of the lower classes, moderation in avarice and greed.

This equality is deemed by many a mere speculative chimera which never can be reduced to practice. But, if the abuse is inevitable, does it follow that we ought not try at least to regulate it? It is precisely because the force of circumstances tends always to destroy equality that the force of legislation must always tend to maintain it.

But these general objects of all good institutions must be moderated in every country by local circumstances, arising from the situation of the place and the character of its inhabitants; and on this account every people must have its peculiar institutions, which, though perhaps not in itself the best of all possible systems, may be the best for that particular State. For example, is your soil sterile and ungrateful, or your country too confined for its inhabitants? Turn your attention to industry and the arts, that you may exchange their productions for the commodities you are in need of. On the other hand, do you occupy rich valleys and fertile hills, and in a fruitful country want people? Bestow all your care on agriculture, which is friendly to population, and chase away the arts, which complete the depopulating of a country by crowding together its few inhabitants on certain spots.[3] If your residence is established on the extensive and commodious shores of the ocean, cover that ocean with your shipping, and cultivate navigation and commerce: you will have a short but glorious existence. Or does the sea find nothing on your coast to wash but almost inaccessible rocks? If so, continue to subsist on fish, and be for ever rude; you will live in greater tranquillity,

[2] If you wish to give consistency to the State, bring these two extremes as near as possible towards each other, and allow of neither excessive wealth nor beggary. These two states, naturally inseparable, are dangerous alike to the common welfare; the one gives birth to the favourers of tyranny, the other to tyrants, and they traffic between them with the public liberty; the one buys it, and the other sells it.

[3] "Every branch of external commerce," says M. d'A. [the Marquis d'Argenson], "affords but a fallacious advantage to a kingdom in general: it may enrich some individuals, or even some towns; but the nation at large gains nothing by it, and the people are not the better for it."

better perhaps, and certainly more happy. In one word, besides the general maxims of legislation which apply to all, there are particular circumstances confined to each people which must influence their application in a particular way, and render their legislation proper only for themselves. Thus we see that the Hebrews formerly, and the Arabs in later times, have had religion for their principal object; the Athenians, literature; Tyre and Carthage, commerce; Rhodes, her marine; Sparta, war; and Rome, virtue. The author of *The Spirit of the Laws*[4] has shown in a multitude of examples with what art the legislator directs the constitution towards each of these objects.

The constitution of a State is rendered most solid and durable when what is proper is so much attended to that the natural relations and the laws mutually agree on every point, and the latter, as it were, but assure, accompany, and correct the former. But if the legislator, mistaken in his object, acts on a principle different from that which arises from the nature of things, if the one tends to servitude and the other to liberty, the one to the increase of wealth and the other to population, or one to peace and the other to conquests, the laws will be insensibly weakened, the constitution altered, and the State kept in continual agitation until it is destroyed or changed, and invincible nature has resumed her sway.

CHAPTER XII

OF THE DIVISION OF THE LAWS

FOR WELL ORDERING the whole, and giving the best possible form to public affairs, there are various relations to be considered: first, the entire body acting upon itself — that is to say, the relations of the whole to the whole, or the Sovereign to the State; and this relation is produced by the relations of the intermediary terms, as we shall see hereafter.

The laws which regulate this relation are named "political laws," and also "fundamental laws," a title they have some right to if they are wise ones. For there can be for every State but one good system,

[4] [Montesquieu; see footnote, p. 36.]

and the people who have been fortunate enough to find that out should adhere to it; but, if a bad one has been adopted, wherefore should they regard as fundamental those laws which prevent them from being good? Besides, in any case, the people are masters, and may change even the best laws; for, if that body is disposed to injure itself, who has a right to prevent it?

The second relation is that which subsists between the different members or to the entire body; in the first instance, this relation should be as little, and in the second as great, as possible; so that each citizen should be perfectly independent of each of his fellow citizens, but very dependent on the city: effects which are always produced by the same cause; for it is only the power of the State that secures the liberty of its members. From this second relation arise civil laws.

There is a third relation between men and the law, that of disobedience to its penalty; this gives rise to the establishment of criminal laws, which, at bottom, are not so much a distinct species of law as the sanction behind all the other laws.

To these three sorts of laws there must be united a fourth, which is the most important of all, and is not inscribed on brass or marble, but in the hearts of the citizens. This makes the true constitution of the State; its powers increase by time; and when all other laws become feeble or even extinct, this reanimates them or supplies their place. This preserves among a people the true spirit of their institution, and substitutes insensibly the force of habit for that of authority. I speak of manners and morals, customs, and more than all, of opinions; these are means unknown to our political thinkers, but on which the success of everything else depends. To them the great legislator directs his secret care, though he appears to confine his attention to particular laws, which are only the curve of the arch, while manners and morals, slower to form, will become at last the immovable key-stone.

Of these different classes of laws, the political, which constitute the form of government, are the only ones that relate to my subject.

BOOK III

Before I speak of the different forms of government, I shall endeavour to fix the precise sense of this word, which has not hitherto been very well explained.

CHAPTER I

OF GOVERNMENT IN GENERAL

I WARN the reader that this chapter requires to be read very seriously, and that I am unacquainted with any art which can make the subject clear to those who will not bestow on it their serious attention.

Every free act must be produced by the concurrence of two causes: the one moral, that is to say, the will which must resolve upon the act, the other physical, that is to say, the power which must execute it. When I go towards an object, it is necessary, in the first place, that I should will to go; and, secondly, that my feet should bear me. If a paralytic person should will to go, and an active man should not will, both would remain where they were. The body politic has the same moving forces: and we find equally in it, as in the natural body, both force and will; the latter distinguished by the name of "legislative power," and the former by that of "executive power." Nothing is or should be done without their concurrence.

We have seen that the legislative power belongs to the people, and can belong to that body only. It is easy to see, on the contrary, by the principles already established, that the executive power cannot belong to the generality as legislator or Sovereign, because that power consists only in individual acts, which are not to be performed by the law, and consequently neither by the Sovereign, all whose acts must be laws.

It is therefore necessary that the public force should have an agent of its own which shall unite and apply that force according to the direction of the general will, to serve as the means of communication between the State and the Sovereign, and to form a sort of public person, in which, as in a man, the union of mind and body should be found. This is the reason why the government in a State is generally, and very improperly, confounded with the Sovereign, of which it is but the minister.

What then is that government? An intermediate body established between the subjects and the Sovereign, for their mutual correspondence, charged with the execution of the laws, and the maintenance of both civil and political liberty.

The members of this body are denominated "magistrates" or "kings," that is to say, "governors"; and the body collectively takes the name of "prince."[1] Thus those who think that the act by which a people submit themselves to their chiefs is not a contract have good foundation for their opinion. That act is certainly no more than a commission, an employment, under which, simply as officers of the Sovereign, the members of government exercise in the name of the Sovereign the power delegated to them, and which may be limited, modified, or recalled at the pleasure of the Sovereign, the alienation of such a right being incompatible with the nature of the social body, and contrary to the end of association.

I therefore give the name of "government" or "supreme administration" to the justifiable exercise of the executive power; and "prince" or "magistrate" to the man or body charged with that administration.

It is in government that those intermediate powers are found whose connections constitute that of the whole with the whole, or of the Sovereign with the State. One can represent this last relation as that between the extreme terms of a continuous proportion of which the mean proportional is government. The government receives from the Sovereign the orders which it transmits to the people; and, to hold the State in proper balance, it is necessary, when everything is considered, to keep upon an equality the power of the government, taken in itself, and the power of the citizens, who are sovereigns in one view and subjects in another.

Further, not one of these three states can be altered without instantly destroying the proportion. If the Sovereign wants to govern, or if the magistrate wants to make laws, or if the subjects refuse to

[1] At Venice they apply to the College [of government] the title of "Most Serene Prince," even when the Doge is not present.

obey, disorder succeeds regularity; and, as force and will can then no longer act in concert, the State is dissolved, and must of course fall into despotism or anarchy. Finally, as there can be but one mean proportional between each relation, there cannot possibly be more than one good government in a State. But, as a thousand events may change the relations of a people, not only may different systems of government be good for different peoples, but for the same people at different periods.

In order to give an idea of the different relations which one extreme bears to another, I shall take as an example the number of a people, which is a relation most easy to express.

We will suppose that the State is composed of ten thousand citizens. The Sovereign must be taken collectively and as a body; but each member, in his quality of a subject, must be regarded as an individual. Thus the Sovereign is to the subject as ten thousand are to one; that is, each member of the State has but a ten-thousandth part of the sovereign authority, though he is entirely subjected to it. When the people amount to one hundred thousand, the situation of the subject does not change, but each is equally under the entire authority of the laws, while his vote is reduced to the hundred-thousandth part, and has ten times less influence in the institution of the laws. Thus, as the subject remains always one, the Sovereign's proportional power increases according to the increased number of citizens. From whence it follows that liberty is diminished by the enlargement of the State.

When I speak of the relation increasing, I mean that it removes further from equality. Thus the greater the proportion is in the acceptation of geometricians, the less proportion there is according to the common idea: for in the first instance it is estimated by its quantity, and is measured by the quotient; and in the second, considered according to its identity, it is estimated by similarity.

The less the private wills are related to the general will, that is, manners and morals to laws, the more the restraining power should be augmented. Therefore, the government, that it may be adequate to the duty required from it, should be made strong in proportion to the number of the people.

On the other hand, as the increasing size of the State presents to the depositaries of the public authority greater temptation and opportunity to abuse their power, the greater force it is necessary to give the government for the purpose of controlling the people, the more should the power of the Sovereign be augmented, that it may control the government. I do not speak here of absolute force, but of force as it relates to the different parts of the State.

It follows from this double relation that the continued proportion which ought to subsist between the Sovereign, the prince, and the people, is not an arbitrary idea, but a necessary consequence of the nature of the body politic. It also follows that one of the extremes — the people in their capacity of subjects — being fixed and represented by unity, the simple proportion must, whenever the duplicate proportion is increased or diminished, increase or diminish accordingly, and the mean term consequently changes. It is evident from this that one unique and absolute arrangement of government would not be proper for every State, but that there can be as many governments different in nature as there are States of degrees of greatness.

Those who wish to turn this system into ridicule will probably tell me that in order to find this mean proportional and establish a body of government, there is nothing to be done, according to my account, but to take the square root of the number of people. I reply that I only made use of a given number by way of example, and that the proportion I speak of cannot be ascertained so much by the number of men as, in general, by the degree of activity, which depends on a multitude of causes; and that, though I employed the terms of geometry in order to express my meaning in fewer words, I am not ignorant that geometrical precision has no place in moral quantities.

Government is on a small scale what the body politic is on an enlarged one. It is a moral person endowed with certain faculties, active like the Sovereign, passive like the State, and which may be analyzed into other similar relations. From this consequently is born a new proportion, and still another within it, according to the arrangement of the tribunals, and so on to that indivisible term, a single chief, or supreme magistrate, which can be represented, in the midst of this progression, as the unity between the fractional and the ordinal series.

But, without embarrassing ourselves with this multiplication of terms, let us be content to consider government as a new body in the

State, distinct from the people and the Sovereign, and forming an intermediate link to connect them.

There is this essential difference between the State and the government: the former is self-existent, and the existence of the latter depends entirely on the Sovereign. Thus the ruling will of the prince neither is nor ought to be anything more than the general will or the law; his force is only the public force concentrated in his hands: if he attempts to execute on his own authority any absolute and independent act, the chain which combines the whole relaxes immediately. And if at last the private will of the prince is more active than the will of the Sovereign, and the public force in his hands is employed to enforce obedience to this private will, so that there are in effect two sovereigns, the one by right, and the other in fact, at that moment the social union ceases, and the body politic is dissolved.

It is, however, necessary that the government should so far have a real existence and life as to be distinguishable from the body of the State; in order that all its members should be able to act in concert and work for the end for which it was instituted, it must have a particular *self*, a sensibility common to its members, and a force and will sufficient for its preservation. This distinct existence supposes assemblies and councils, a power to deliberate and resolve, rights, titles, and privileges which belong to the prince alone, and which render the situation of a magistrate more honourable in proportion as it is more laborious. The great difficulty of forming a body of government lies in ordering this subaltern whole within the whole in such a manner that the general constitution may not be altered by giving too much strength to this part; that the particular force necessary for preserving itself may be kept distinct from the public force which is necessary to preserve the State; and, in fine, that on every occasion the government may be sacrificed to the people, and not the people to the government.

Further, though government is an artificial body, formed by, and dependent on, another body, likewise artificial, and though in some degree its existence is borrowed and inferior, yet it can act with more or less strength and activity, and it may be said to enjoy a greater or less degree of robustness and health. Finally, without swerving entirely from those ends for which it was instituted, it may deviate from it more or less, in accordance with the manner in which it is constituted.

It is in consequence of all these differences that the various relations between the government and the body of the State arise, in accordance with the accidental and particular relations by which the State itself is changed. For often the very best government in itself will become the worst, if the relations in which it stands have changed in accordance with the faults of the body politic to which it belongs.

CHAPTER II

Of the Principles Which Constitute the Different Forms of Government

To explain the general cause of these differences, it is necessary to distinguish the principle from the government, as I have already distinguished the State from the Sovereign.

The body of the magistracy may be composed of a greater or less number of members. We have said that the relation which the Sovereign has to the subjects is increased by an increase of population; and, by an obvious analogy, we can say that the relation of government to the magistrates is the same.

But the total force of the government, being always the force of the State, cannot vary: from whence it follows that the more of this force it employs on its own members, the less there will remain to expend on the whole people.

Therefore, the more numerous the body of magistrates is, the weaker the government must be. As this is a fundamental maxim, it will be proper to explain it clearly.

There are in the person of a magistrate three essentially different wills: first, his private will as an individual, which points only to his own interest; secondly, his will as a magistrate, which he has in common with the other magistrates, which regards only the interest of the prince, and may be properly called the will of the whole body of which he is a member,[1] and which is *general* with respect to government,

---

[1] [Hereinafter referred to as the "group-will."]

but *private* with respect to the State of which the government makes a part; his third will is the will of the people, or the sovereign will, which is general, both in regard to the State as the whole and to the government considered as part of the whole.

In perfect legislation, the private or individual will should be null, the will of the body of the government very subordinate, and consequently the general or sovereign will always predominant over all and solely directing all the rest.

According to the natural order, however, these different wills become more active in proportion as they are concentrated. Thus, the general will is always weakest, that of the magistracy stronger, and the private will the strongest of all: so that, in the government, each member is first himself, then a magistrate, and then a citizen — a direct inversion of that order of things which the social order requires.

But let us suppose the government in the hands of one man: then the private will and the group-will are perfectly united, and the latter consequently enjoys the highest degree of power it is capable of possessing. But since it is on the degree reached by the will that the use of force depends, and since the absolute force of the government does not vary, it must follow that the most active government is that of one man.

But if we were to unite the government to the legislative authority, make the Sovereign the prince, and all the citizens magistrates, then the group-will, confounded with the general will, would lose its own activity, yet leave the private will in all its force. Thus the government, though always possessing the same absolute force, would be at its minimum of relative force or activity.

All this is incontestable, and may be still further proved. We see, for instance, that the magistrate is more active in the body to which he belongs than the citizen is in his, and that, consequently, the private will has much more influence in the acts of the government than in those of the Sovereign; for each magistrate is almost continually employed in some function of government, while each citizen, taken singly, has none of the functions of the sovereignty to perform. Furthermore, as the State increases, there is an increase in its real strength, though not in proportion to its increased extent; but while the State remains the same, it would be useless to augment the number of magistrates, since the real force of the government could not thereby be augmented; for it can have none to employ but that of the State, the dimension of which is always equal. Thus the relative power, or the activity of the government, would be considerably diminished, without its absolute or real force being augmented.

Furthermore, it is certain that public business is retarded in proportion to the number of persons employed in transacting it; that they often err by attending too much to prudence, and not leaving enough to fortune, by which means opportunities are lost; and that the time they spend in deliberating would, if properly improved, often ensure the object of deliberation.

I have just proved that government is weakened in proportion to the multiplication of magistrates; and I have already proved that the restraining power must be augmented as the people become more numerous. From this it follows that the proportion of magistrates to the government must be exactly the reverse of the proportion of subjects to the Sovereign; that is, the more the State extends, the more the government must be compressed, so that the number of chiefs may diminish as the number of the people increases.

I here speak only of the relative force of government, and not of its rectitude; for, on the other hand, the more magistrates there are, the nearer the will of the magistracy must approach the general will; while, under one single magistrate, this same will of the group is, as I have before remarked, only a private will. Thus, what is lost on one side is gained on the other, and the great art of the legislator is to fix the exact point where the force and the will of government, always bearing a reciprocal proportion, can be combined in the manner most advantageous to the State.

CHAPTER III

OF THE DIVISION OF GOVERNMENTS

WE HAVE SEEN in the preceding chapter that the different forms of government are distinguished by the number of members which compose them; we shall now see how governments are divided.

The Sovereign can commit the charge of government to all the people, or to the greater part of the people, in such a manner that there will be more citizen-magistrates than simple private citizens. This form of government is called a "democracy."

The Sovereign can also confine the government in the hands of a small number, so that there may be more private citizens than magistrates; and this form is denominated an "aristocracy."

Finally, the whole government may be concentrated in the hands of one magistrate from whom all the other magistrates shall hold their power. This is the most common form, and is known by the name of "monarchy," or "royal government."

All these forms of government, but especially the two first, are susceptible of more or less, and even of great variation. Democracy may include all the people, or be confined to half. Aristocracy may take in half the people, or be centered in the smallest number, indeterminately. Even royalty may be divided. Sparta had, by the rules of her constitution, always two kings; and the Roman Empire is known to have had eight emperors at once without the Empire being divided. So that each form of government has some point which runs it into the next; and we see that, under the three comprehensive names of "democracy," "aristocracy," and "monarchy," government may be modelled into as many different forms as there are citizens in the State. Nay, further still: the same government may in some respects be subdivided into different parts, one part administered in one manner, and another in another, and, from the combination of all the three forms, a multitude of mixed forms may proceed, each of which may be again multipliable by all the simple forms.

It has been the subject of much dispute in all ages which of the three forms of government is the best, without considering that each may be the best in certain cases, and the worst in others.

If it be necessary in States that the number of supreme magistrates should be in inverse proportion to the number of citizens, then, consequently, the democratic government is most suitable to small States, the aristocratic to those of the middle size, and the monarchical to the greatest. This rule immediately follows from the principle laid down. But it is impossible to say how many circumstances may produce exceptions.

CHAPTER IV

OF DEMOCRACY

THE POWER that makes the laws knows better than any other person how they ought to be executed and how interpreted. It seems from this that the best constitution would be that where the legislative and executive powers are united: but that very union is the thing which renders this government so unsatisfactory in certain respects, because those things which ought to be distinguished are not, and because the prince and the Sovereign, then the same, form in a manner a government without a government.

It is not good for the power that makes the laws to execute them; neither would it be proper that the body of the people should turn their eyes from general views to fix them on particular objects. Nothing is more dangerous than private interest having any influence on public affairs, and the abuse of the laws by the government is a lesser evil than the corruption of the legislator, which is an infallible consequence of such private views. In such a case, the very substance of the State is changed, and all reformation becomes impossible. A people who never abused the powers of government would never abuse independence; a people who always governed well would have no need to be governed.

Taking the word "democracy" in its strict sense, perhaps there never did, and never will, exist such a government. It is against the natural order that the greater number should govern, and the smaller number be governed. It cannot be imagined that the chief part of the people should be always assembled for the discharge of public affairs, and it is evident that commissioners cannot be appointed to govern without the form of administration changing.

In fact, I believe it may be laid down as a principle that, when the functions of government are divided among a number of tribunals, the fewer in number will sooner or later acquire the greatest authority, if it were for no other reason than because affairs will be transacted with greatest ease and expedition in fewest hands, which naturally brings them control of affairs.

Besides, how many circumstances must conspire to make such a government possible!   First, the State must be a very small one, where the people can easily assemble, and where each citizen can easily know all the others; there must, in the second place, be great simplicity of manners to prevent a multiplicity of affairs and those tedious discussions which are the consequence of them; and there must also be much equality in the rank and fortunes of all the citizens, or there will not be equality of rights and authority for long; finally there must be little or no luxury, for whether luxury be considered as the effect of riches, or as the incitement to covet them, it corrupts at once both the wealthy and the poor, the one by its possession, the other by the desire of possessing; it betrays the nation into effeminate softness, and debases it by vanity; and it takes away all the citizens from the State by making them subservient to each other, and all the slaves of opinion.

This is the reason why a celebrated author[1] has made virtue the principle on which a republic must be founded; because all these circumstances could never subsist without her ruling influence.   But this fine genius has not only omitted making the necessary distinctions, but he is not always exact, and sometimes obscure, and he did not perceive that, the sovereign authority being everywhere the same, the same principle must prevail in every well-formed State, though in a greater or less degree, according to its form of government.

I must yet add that there is no government so subject to civil wars and internal agitations as the democratic or popular one, because there is not one which has so strong and so continual a tendency to change its form, or which needs more vigilance and courage to maintain it.   This is the constitution which, more than any other, requires the citizen to arm himself with strength and constancy, and to repeat every day of his life what a virtuous Palatine[2] said in the Diet of Poland: *Mal pericolosam libertatem quam quietum servitium.*[3]

If there were a nation of gods they might be governed by a democracy.   So perfect a government will not agree with men.

[1] [Montesquieu, *The Spirit of Laws*, Bk. III, chap. 3.]
[2] The Palatine of Posen, father of the King of Poland, Duke of Lorraine.
[3] [Better liberty with danger than peace with slavery.]

CHAPTER V

OF ARISTOCRACY

WE HAVE HERE two moral persons entirely distinct from each other: the government, and the Sovereign; and, consequently, two general wills: the one in relation to all the citizens, the other for the members of the administration only. Thus, although the government can regulate its internal policy as it pleases, it can never speak to the people but in the name of the Sovereign, that is, in the name of the people themselves — a circumstance which must never be forgotten.

The aristocratic form of government prevailed in the first societies. The heads of the families deliberated among themselves on public affairs, while the younger people submitted without reluctance to the authority of experience. Hence the names of "priest," "elder," "senator," and "geronte."[1] This mode of government still prevails among the savages of North America, and they are very well governed.

But in proportion as the inequality produced by institutions came to dominate over natural inequality, the rich or the powerful[2] were preferred to the aged, and the aristocracy became elective. Finally, the power transmitted with the property of the father to the children rendered some families patrician, made the government hereditary, and introduced into the senate men only twenty years old.

There are, therefore, three sorts of aristocracy: the natural, the elective, and the hereditary. The first is suited only to simple peoples; the third is the worst of all governments. The second, which is true aristocracy, is the best.

Besides the advantage of two distinct powers, this last species of aristocracy has that of choosing its members; for in popular governments all the citizens are born magistrates; but this last form confines their number, and none can enjoy the magisterial power but by election,[3] by which means probity, knowledge, experience, and all the

---

[1] [honoured old man.]

[2] It is clear that the word "optimates," with the ancients, did not mean the best, but the most powerful.

[3] It is of infinite consequence to a State that the election of magistrates should be regulated by law; for, by leaving it to the will of the prince, an hereditary aris-

other qualities which claim public preference and esteem, are so many new guarantees of judicious government.

And, more than this, the public assemblies are better conducted; affairs are better discussed, and dispatched with more order and diligence; and the credit of the State is more firmly supported with foreigners by venerable senators than by an unknown or contemptible multitude.

In short, it is the best and most natural rule that the wisest should govern the multitude, when there is an assurance that they will govern for its welfare, and not for their own. It is not necessary to increase unnecessarily the springs of government, or to employ twenty thousand men to do what might be even better done by one hundred chosen men. But we must not forget that the interest of this body begins to direct the public force less under the rule of the general will, and that there is an inevitable propensity to take away from the laws a part of the executive power.

With regard to the circumstances particularly favourable to this form of government, it does not require the State to be so small, or the people to be so innocent and upright, that the execution of the laws immediately follows from the public will, as in a good democracy. Neither should the nation be so extensive as to give opportunity to those chiefs who are dispersed for the purpose of governing its provinces to play the Sovereign in their own departments, and to begin to make themselves independent in order finally to become masters.

But if aristocracy may subsist without all the virtues indispensable in popular government, it requires others which are peculiarly its own, such as moderation in the rich, and contentment in the poor; for a rigorous equality would seem to be improper in a State so governed; it was not found even at Sparta.

Furthermore, if the aristocratic system allows of a certain inequality of fortune, the reason is that in general the administration of public affairs may be confided to persons who can best give them all their time, and not, as Aristotle pretends, so that the rich may be always preferred.[4] On the contrary, it is important that an opposite choice tocracy will certainly be established, as was the case in the Republics of Venice and Berne. The first of these States has in consequence fallen long since into decay; and the latter, which is preserved by the extreme wisdom of its senate, stands an honourable but a very dangerous exception to a general rule.

[4] [Compare Aristotle's *Politics*, Bk. VI, chap. 6.]

sometimes teach the people that merit has a much stronger and more important claim to public favour and confidence than wealth can possibly create.

CHAPTER VI

OF MONARCHY

WE HAVE hitherto considered the prince as a moral and collective person, united by the force of the laws, and depositary in the State of the executive power. We must now consider this power as gathered in the hands of a natural person, of a real man who alone has a right to dispose of it according to the laws. This person is called a "monarch," or "king."

As against other forms of administration, where a collective being represents an individual, here an individual represents a collective being, so that the moral unity which constitutes the prince is at the same time a physical unity, in which all the faculties that the law unites in the other with so much effort are found naturally united.

Thus, the will of the people, the will of the prince, the public force of the State, and the particular force of the government, all respond to the same mover, all the springs of the machine are regulated by the same hand, all act together for effecting the same purpose; the movement of no one part clashes with or impedes any other; and it is impossible to imagine any kind of constitution in which less effort would produce a more considerable action. Archimedes, sitting quietly on the beach and drawing a large vessel afloat, represents to me an able monarch, governing great States from his closet and giving motion to all, while he himself seems to remain immovable.

But if there is no government which possesses more vigour than monarchy, there is not one in which the private will has greater influence, or domineers more easily over the others: all moves, it is true, to the same end; but that end is not the public felicity, and even the force of the administration is turned incessantly to the prejudice of the State.

Kings are all desirous of being absolute, and they are told from all quarters that the most certain way of becoming so is to gain the affections of the people. This is a fine maxim, and even very true in some respects. Unfortunately, they will always laugh at it at court. The power which is derived from the attachment of the people is undoubtedly the greatest; but it is precarious, and conditional; princes will never be content with it. The best king wishes to possess the power of being evil, if he pleases, without ceasing to be master. A political preacher may tell the kings that the force of the people is their force, and that it is to the monarchs' greatest interest that the people should be flourishing, numerous, and formidable; they know very well that that is untrue. It is to the king's personal interest to keep the people weak and miserable, that they may want the power to resist. I grant that, if subjects were always perfectly submissive, it would be the prince's interest to make them powerful, because, as their power would be his, he might employ it to render himself formidable to the neighbouring states. As this is, however, but a secondary and subordinate consideration, and as the two suppositions, of a people being able to resist the will of a tyrant, and of their continuing entirely obedient to his will, are incompatible, we must of course conclude that princes will ever give the preference to that maxim which will be most immediately useful to them. Samuel represented this in the strongest manner to the Hebrews, and Machiavelli has proved it by incontestable evidence. Indeed, while he pretended to be giving lessons to kings, he gave the noblest lesson to the people. *The Prince* of Machiavelli is the book of republicans.[1]

We have found, on general grounds, that monarchy is proper only for an extensive State; and we shall be more convinced as we enquire into it in itself. In proportion as the members of the administrative body increase, the relation of the prince to his subjects diminishes, and they all draw towards equality, so that the ratio is one to one, or absolute equality, in a democracy. This ratio increases in proportion

---

[1] Machiavelli was an honest man and a good citizen; but, attached as he was to the court of the Medici, he was forced, in the midst of the oppression of his country, to disguise his love of liberty. The choice of his execrable hero [Cæsar Borgia] alone is enough to show his secret intention; and the opposition of the maxims contained in *The Prince* to those in his *Discourses on Livy* and in his *History of Florence* shows that this profound political thinker has only had superficial or corrupt readers up to now. The court of Rome has strictly prohibited his book: I can well believe it; it is that court which he most clearly describes.

as the government is smaller in members, and gains its *maximum* when the government is in the hands of one single man. But then there is too great a disparity between the prince and the people, and the State feels the want of some connecting chain. Intermediate degrees of rank are found necessary, and princes, grandees, and nobility are created to fill them. But nothing of this kind is proper in a little State, which is ruined by all these distinctions of rank.

It is difficult for great States to be well governed, and all the more difficult when they are under the government of one man; and everyone knows what happens once a king governs through deputies.

There is one essential and certain evil attendant on monarchical governments which must always render them inferior to republics: while in the latter men of talents and information, whose abilities do honour to the choice that selects them, are chosen by the public voice to fill the highest offices, those who reach the highest offices in a monarchy are too frequently a disgrace to their station. They are, in general, men who have wound themselves into favour by knavery, tattling, and intrigue, and who, making their way to power by those superficial qualities that please a giddy court, have no sooner attained it than they discover to the public their unfitness to hold the situation. The people are much less often mistaken in their choice than the prince is; and you as seldom find a fool at the head of a republican government as you do a man of true merit in the cabinet of a prince. Thus, when, by some happy chance, a man of talents, born to govern, is placed at the helm of an almost sinking monarchy which has been directed by these pretty ministers, it is astonishing to see the resources he opens, and his ministry is one of the great events which form an epoch in the history of a country.

In order to have a monarchical State well governed, its greatness and extent should be proportioned to the genius of the prince who governs it. It is easier to conquer than to rule. Had we but a sufficient lever, we might, even with a finger, lift the world; but it would require the shoulders of Hercules to support it afterwards. However little a State may be, the prince is almost always too little for it. But even when the State is too small for its chief, which very rarely happens, still we find it equally ill-governed, because then the chief, pursuing continually his great purposes, forgets the interests of the people, and renders them no less unhappy by the abuse of his superabundant talents than a weak chief does by the want of those which nature has denied him. It would therefore be proper for a kingdom to expand or compress itself at the accession of every prince, and as nearly as possible to adapt its limits to his capacity; but as the talents of a senate are less subject to change, the State it governs may have its fixed boundaries, and the administration never suffers by it.

The most sensible inconvenience attending the government of a single man is the want of that continuous succession which forms in the two others an uninterrupted chain. A king dies, and there must be another; if he is to be elected, the interregnum leaves a dangerous interval, which often proves very turbulent; and unless the citizens have more disinterestedness and integrity than is common under such governments, corruption mixes with the spirit of cabal. The chief to whom the State has sold itself will probably sell it in his turn, and indemnify himself at the expense of the weak for the gold which the powerful have extorted from him. Thus, sooner or later, all must become venal under such a ministry, and the peace which may then be enjoyed under a king is worse than the disorders of the interregnum.

What has been done to prevent these evils? Crowns have been made hereditary in certain families; and an order of succession established which puts an end to all disputes which arise upon the death of kings; that is, the inconvenience of a regency has been substituted for that of an election, apparent tranquillity preferred to a wise administration, and the danger of having children, fools, or monsters become kings has been chosen rather than to have disputes about the choice of good ones; men did not perceive that, by exposing themselves to the dangers of such an alternative, the chances were all against them. One great evil of hereditary monarchies is strikingly shown in the very sensible reply of the younger Dionysius, when his father, reproaching him for some base action, said, "I never set you the example." "No," answered his son, "your father never was a king."

Everything conspires to deprive a man who is brought up to command others of the use of his reason as well as of his principles of justice. We are told, indeed, that much pains are employed to instruct a young prince in the art of reigning: but we do not find that they profit by this education. It might be better if they were first taught the art of obeying. Those kings of whom history makes the most honourable mention were not trained in the expectation of wearing a crown; the science of governing is one about which those persons always know the least who have learned too much of it, and which is generally better acquired by persons more accustomed to obeying than to commanding. *Nam utilissimus idem ac brevissimus bonarum mala-rumque rérum delectus, cogitare quid aut nolueris sub alio principe, aut volueris.*[2]

One consequence of this want of coherence is the changeableness of royal government, which, being sometimes regulated by one plan, and sometimes by another, according to the disposition of the king who reigns or of those who reign for him, cannot long have one deter-mined object to pursue or a consistent course of conduct to follow: and the consequent variation of conduct always makes the State waver from maxim to maxim and from project to project, an evil which does not exist in a democracy or an aristocracy, where the prince is always the same. It is, therefore, evident that, in general, if there is more cunning in a court, there is more wisdom in a senate, and that republics pursue their ends by a more regular and better considered course; which indeed cannot be done where every change of ministry produces a revolution in the State: for it is a maxim with all ministers, and with nearly all kings, to take a path exactly contrary to that of their predecessor.

From this want of coherence in royal government, we may draw the solution of a sophism very familiar to royalist political thinkers; not only do they compare civil to domestic government, and the prince to the father of a family — an error already confuted — but they give liberally to that magistrate all the virtues he ought to have, and suppose him always the very thing he ought to be. By the aid of this supposition, royal government must appear evidently the best of all, because it is incontestably the strongest, and only wants a group-will more conformable to the general will to give it superiority over all others.

But if, according to Plato,[3] a man qualified by nature to be a king is very rare, in what a variety of circumstances must nature and fortune concur to crown him! And, if royal education necessarily corrupts

[2] Tacitus, *Histories*, I, 16. [The best as well as the shortest way to find out what is good and what is bad is to consider what you would have wished to happen or not to happen if there had been some other prince than you.]

[3] In *The Statesman*.

those who receive it, what can we hope for from a succession of men that are duly qualified for reigning? Those persons must therefore be very willing to deceive themselves who confound royal government with the government of a good king. To know what this government is in itself we must first view it under weak or dissolute princes; for they will accede to the throne weak or dissolute, or will imbibe their vices from it.

These difficulties have not escaped our writers; but they have not been bothered by them. They propose a remedy which is simply to obey without murmuring; God has given bad kings in his anger, and we must bear their oppressions as the chastisements of Heaven.[4] Discourse of this kind is undoubtedly very edifying; but I believe it would do better from the pulpit than in a book on politics. What should we say to a physician who promises miracles, but whose whole art is to exhort the sick man to be patient? We know very well that a bad government must be endured when we are under it. The question should be to find a good one.

CHAPTER VII

OF MIXED GOVERNMENTS

PROPERLY SPEAKING, there are no simple governments. A single chief must have subordinate magistrates; a popular government cannot do without a chief. Thus we see that, in the partition of executive power, there is always a gradation from the greater number to the lesser, with the difference that sometimes the greater number depend upon the lesser and sometimes the lesser number depend on the greater.

Sometimes there is an equal division, when the constituent parts are mutually dependent, as in the government of England; or when the authority of each part is independent but imperfect, as in Poland. This last form is bad, because the government wants unity, and the State wants a connecting bond.

[4] [For a statement of the philosophy of divine-right monarchy, see Bossuet's *Politique tirèe de l'écriture sainte*, written about 1670, and published in 1709.]

If I were asked which is the best form of government, the simple or the mixed, a question that has been strongly debated by political thinkers, I should answer as I have already done with respect to all the other forms of government.

The simple government is the best in itself because it is simple. But when the executive power does not depend sufficiently on the legislative, that is, when the relation between the prince and the Sovereign is closer than that between the people and the prince, the want of due proportion must be remedied by dividing the government; for all the parts of government have then no less authority over the subjects, and their division will render them less formidable with respect to the Sovereign.

The establishment of intermediate magistrates would also prevent this disadvantage, for, while they left the government entire, they would balance the two powers and maintain their respective rights. By this means the government is not mixed, it is tempered.

The opposite evil will find its remedy by similar measures; that is, when the government is too much relaxed, by erecting tribunals to concentrate it. This is practised in all democracies. In the first instance, the government is divided to weaken it, and, in the second, to give it new force; for the *maxima* of both strength and weakness are found in simple governments, while the mixed ones produce a mean strength.

CHAPTER VIII

That Every Form of Government would not be Proper in Every Country

LIBERTY not being a fruit that every climate will produce, it is not within the abilities of all peoples. The more we consider this principle established by Montesquieu, the more we perceive its truth; and those who attempt to controvert it only afford fresh opportunity of finding new proofs of its justice.

In all governments whatever, the public person consumes but never produces anything. From whence then comes the substance consumed by it? From the labour of its members. It is the surplus from individuals that furnishes the necessary supply for the public person. We may therefore conclude that the civil State can only subsist while the labour of men produces more than their own needs require.

This surplus varies in different countries. In some it may be considerable, in others moderate, in others nothing, and in some it may even be negative. This must depend on the fertility of the climate, on the sort of labour which the ground requires to cultivate it, on the nature of its productions, on the strength of its inhabitants, on the greater or less consumption which they require, and on a variety of other circumstances.

On the other hand, all governments are not of the same nature; some are more, others less, devouring; and the difference arises from this principle, that public contributions become more oppressive the farther they are removed from the source from whence they were drawn. It is not by the amount of public taxes that we must judge how far they are burdensome to the people on whom they are assessed, but by the path they have to take to come back into the same hands from whence they came. When the circulation is prompt and well-established, it does not matter whether much or little is paid; the people will be always rich, and the finances flourishing. On the contrary, let the taxes paid by the people be ever so trifling, if that trifle never flows back into their hands, the continual drain must exhaust them: the State will be always poor and the people beggars.

It is evident from these truths that, as the distance between the people and the government increases, the tributes paid by the former must become more oppressive: thus, in a democracy, the burden of taxes is little felt; in the aristocracy, more; and in a monarchy, their weight is heaviest. Monarchy is therefore suited to none but opulent nations; aristocracy to those States which are moderately rich and extensive; and democracy to such States as are both small and poor.

In fact, the more we reflect, the more we find the difference between free States and monarchies to be this: in the first, all is employed for the purposes of public utility; in the other, public and private forces have a reciprocal effect on one another, and the one grows by weakening the other. In fine, instead of governing its subjects to make them happy, despotism makes them miserable in order to govern them.

It must appear from what has just been said that there are in every climate certain natural causes which seem to mark out the required kind of government, and even the sort of inhabitants that are most proper.

A sterile domain which will not prove grateful to the hand that endeavours to reclaim it must always continue an uncultivated desert, or be at best the abode of savages. The land which will yield only a bare subsistence in return for the labour bestowed upon it must be the habitation of barbarous people; for polity would be there impossible; the ground which affords only a moderate surplus of produce over labour is a proper residence for a free people; while those abundant and fertile domains which give much produce for little labour seem formed to be the seat of monarchical government, in which the luxury of the prince may consume the excess of the super-abundant produce of his subjects; for it is better that the surplus should be absorbed by the government than dissipated by private individuals. I know there are exceptions to this rule; but these very exceptions serve to confirm it, because they sooner or later produce revolutions which return things to their natural order.

We should always distinguish general laws from the particular causes that sometimes limit their effect. Though all the South should be converted into republics, and all the North become despotic States, it would not be less true that, from the influence of climate, warm countries should be the seat of despotism, and cold ones the haunt of barbarous people, while good polity should dwell with the inhabitants of the intermediary regions. I see also that, though this principle be granted, the application of it may be disputed: it may be said that some cold countries are very fertile, and some tropical ones exceedingly barren. But this objection can only weigh with those who do not view the matter in all its aspects. As I have already said, the labour, the power, the consumption, etc., should be taken into account.

Let us suppose that, of two districts equal in extent, the proportion of produce is as five to ten. If the inhabitants of the first consume four parts, and the inhabitants of the second nine parts of such produce, then the surplus of the one will be a fifth, and the surplus of the other a tenth. This shows an inverse proportion to that of their produce, the district which produced only five giving a surplus double that of the district which yielded ten.

It is not a question, however, of a double product, and I believe no person will deny that warm countries are in general more fertile than cold ones. But, for the sake of argument, let us suppose them equal in this respect, and admit that the same extent of land will yield as much in England as in Sicily, and in Poland as in Egypt. Further to the south we should find Africa and the Indies, further to the north, nothing. What a difference there must be in the cultivation, to make the ground afford this equality of produce! In Sicily one need do no more than lightly rake the ground; in England what infinite labour is necessary! And, where a greater number of hands are required to procure the same quantity of produce from the same space of ground, the proportion of surplus must be smaller.

We must also consider that the same number of men do not consume nearly so much in a warm as in a cold country. The climate obliges them to avoid excess in order to preserve health; and those Europeans who pursue there the habits they have formed in their own countries all perish of dysentery and indigestion. "We are," says Chardin,[1] "carnivorous as wolves in comparison with the Asiatics. Some attribute the moderation of the Persians to the scanty cultivation of their country, but I, on the contrary, believe that the country abounds less in provision because the inhabitants require less. If their frugality," he continues, "were an effect of the barrenness of the land, it would only be the poor that subsisted on a scanty portion, instead of that forbearance being, as it now is, universal; and more or less would be consumed in each province according to its fertility, without one general system of abstemiousness prevailing through all the kingdom. The Persians pique themselves greatly on their manner of living, and say that it is easy to judge by their complexions how much more excellent their customs are than those of the Christians. In fact, the Persians have an even complexion; their skins are delicate, smooth, and beautiful; while those of their Armenian subjects, who live after the European manner, are rough and blotched, and their bodies gross and heavy."

[1] [Jean (Sir John) Chardin (1643-1713), who traveled extensively in Persia and India.]

The nearer we approach the Line,[2] the less is required by people to sustain them. They eat almost no meat; rice, Indian corn, curcur, millet, and cassava are their ordinary food. There are millions of men in the Indies whose maintenance may be estimated at even less than a penny a day. Even in Europe we perceive a considerable difference between the appetites of the Northern and Southern peoples. A Spaniard will live a week, for instance, on the dinner of a German. In countries where men are most voracious, the prevalent luxury is that of the table. In England you sit down to an entertainment composed of a profusion of viands; in Italy they regale you with sugar and flowers.

The luxury of dress is also very different in different places. In climates where the transition from one season to another is sudden and extreme, garments are better and simpler; in places where ornament is the only object of dress, they study splendour more than utility; and there even their garments are a luxury. Thus you see every day at Naples, sauntering on the Pausilippeum, men in gold-embroidered coats and nothing else.

The same remark holds good with respect to buildings: magnificence is the only object attended to where nothing is to be apprehended from the air. At Paris and London you desire to be lodged in warm, convenient dwellings; at Madrid you find superb salons, but windows are not even made to shut, and you sleep in a miserable hole.

A third consideration, which cannot fail to have great influence on the second, is that in hot countries the food is much more substantial and succulent. Why are vegetables so much eaten in Italy? Because they are there wholesome, nourishing, and of excellent taste. In France, where the same products are fed by little else but water, they nourish not, and are considered as nothing on the table. Yet they occupy as much ground, and cost as much labour in the cultivation. It is known, from experiments, that the corn of Barbary, inferior in other respects to that of France, yields a greater proportion of flour, and that French corn, in its turn, produces much more than the corn that grows farther northward. We may infer, therefore, that there is a natural and general gradation from the Line to the Pole. Is it not an obvious disadvantage to have from the same quantity of produce so great a deficiency of nutritive virtue?

[2] [The equator.]

To the considerations already mentioned, another very important one may be added, which at once proceeds from them and strengthens them: it is that, though warm countries need fewer inhabitants than cold countries, they are able to support more inhabitants than cold countries. This produces a double surplus, a circumstance always favourable to despotism. The more a fixed number of inhabitants are spread abroad, the more difficult it is for them to revolt, because they cannot concert any plan quickly or secretly, and because it will also be more in the power of government to prevent their designs and cut off their communication.

On the other hand, the usurpations of sovereignty by the government become less practicable in proportion to the number of people who are compressed together: for, when they are drawn within a smaller circle, their chiefs can deliberate together in their closets as securely as the prince in his council chamber, and the multitude may assemble as soon in the squares, as the troops of government can in their quarters. A tyrannical government, therefore, is best secured by having its subjects dispersed, as it acts most forcibly at a distance. Its power, aided by the points of support it establishes, is, like a great lever, efficacious in proportion to the distance it extends.[3] That of the people, on the contrary, possesses its greatest strength when it is most concentrated: it evaporates and is lost by extension, like gunpowder scattered on the ground, which catches fire only grain by grain. The country which is least populous is therefore the most proper situation for a tyrant; ferocious beasts reign only in deserts.

CHAPTER IX

OF THE SIGNS OF A GOOD GOVERNMENT

THE QUESTION, "Which is absolutely the best government?" is as insoluble as it is indeterminate; or, if you wish, there are as many

[3] This does not contradict what I have said, in the ninth chapter of the Second Book, on the inconveniency of great States. It was there a question of the authority of the government over the members, and it is here a question of its force against the subjects. Its scattered members would serve as points of support for action against the people at a distance, but it could have no points of support for direct action against its own members themselves. Thus, in one case, the length of the lever would weaken it, and in the other augment its powers.

replies as there are possible combinations in the absolute and relative situations of nations.

But if it were asked what is the sign of a nation being well- or ill-governed, that would be another matter, and an answer might be given to this question of fact.

It is not answered, however, because each man wants to answer it in his own way. Thus, subjects extol public tranquillity, citizens the personal liberty of individuals; one prefers the security of property, another the security of persons; this man is for the government which is most severe, the other holds that the mildest government is best; one would have crimes punished, another is for preventing them; one man wishes to see his country the terror of all the neighbouring States, another man would rather have it remain ignored; one thinks everything goes on well so long as money circulates freely, another judges it more necessary that the people should have bread. Even if there were agreement on all these and similar points, would we have made any progress? Men have no way of measuring moral quantities precisely, and, even if they were to agree upon the sign of a good government, their ideas of the value that ought to be set upon it would vary greatly.

It is astonishing to me that people can so greatly mistake a sign which is so simple, or that they can be so insincere as not to acknowledge it. What is the end of political association? The preservation and prosperity of its members. And what is the most certain sign that they are preserved and that they prosper? Their numbers and their population. We need seek no further for the sign in dispute. That government is infallibly the best, all other things being equal, under which, without the employment of any external means, without the naturalization of strangers, without receiving any new colonists, the citizens increase and multiply. That is the worst under which they lessen and decay. Calculators, it is now your affair; count, measure, and compare them.[1]

[1] We may judge, by the same principle, of the centuries in which the human race has enjoyed the greatest degree of prosperity. Too much admiration has been given to those in which letters and arts have flourished; and men have not sufficiently considered the hidden object of their culture, or their fatal effect: *Idque apud imperitos humanitas vocabatur, cum pars servitutis esset.* ["Fools called 'humanity' what was part of slavery." (Tacitus, Agricola, 31.)] Shall we never detect the gross selfishness which induces authors to disseminate such maxims?

CHAPTER X

OF THE ABUSE OF GOVERNMENT AND ITS PROPENSITY TO DEGENERATE

JUST AS THE PRIVATE WILL continually acts against the general will, so the government makes an unremitted effort against the Sovereign. The more this effort increases, the more the constitution becomes altered; and there being no will of any other body which, in resisting that of the prince, produces an equilibrium with it, the Sovereign must be at length oppressed by the prince, and the social treaty broken. This innate and inevitable vice tends, from the birth of the body politic, to destroy it, as old age and death do in the human frame.

There are two general ways by which a government degenerates: when it suffers contraction, or when the State is dissolved.

Government suffers contraction when it passes from a greater to a

But let them say what they will, it is false that everything goes well in a State, let its splendour be what it may, if the population decreases, and that a poet has an income of a hundred thousand livres does not make the age he lived in the best that the world ever experienced. In order to judge which ages have been most happy, we should less consider the appearance of tranquillity and repose of chiefs than the well-being of whole nations, and particularly of populous States. A hail-storm may spread desolation through some cantons, but it seldom occasions a general famine. Revolts and civil wars may frighten many chiefs; but they may not prove real misfortunes to the people, who may even have a respite during the struggle between those who seek to tyrannize over them. It is a long continuance in the same situation that makes prosperity or calamity real. When a whole nation lies crushed under the yoke, it is then that all decays, and it is then that their masters can hurl destruction amongst them at will. *Ubi solitudinem faciunt, pacem appellant.* ["Where they make solitude, they call it peace." (Tacitus, *Agricola,* 31.)] When the factions of the chief men in France had arisen to such a height as to agitate the kingdom, and the Coadjutor of Paris judged it necessary to carry a dagger in his pocket every time he went into the Parliament, the French people prospered and increased, and lived in dignity, free and at ease. And Greece formerly flourished in the midst of cruel wars; the blood flowed in torrents, and the country was covered with men. It seemed, says Machiavelli, that amidst a scene of murders, proscriptions, and civil wars, our Republic became more powerful; the virtue, the morality, and the independence of the citizens are more successful in reinforcing the State than all their dissensions are in weakening it. A little agitation gives new vigour to men's minds, and the prosperity of the race depends much more on liberty than peace.

smaller number, as in its passage from democracy to aristocracy, and from aristocracy to royalty. This is the course it is naturally inclined to pursue.[1] If it were to take a retrograde direction, and proceed from the smaller to the greater number, it might be said to relax; but this inverted progress is impossible.

In fact, government never changes its form but when its exhausted energies leave it too weak to support itself. If it becomes still more

[1] The slow and progressive formation of the Republic of Venice in its canals offers a notable example of this succession; and it is very astonishing that, after a space of more than twelve hundred years, the Venetians seem to be still only in the second stage of gradation which commenced with the *Serrar di Consiglio* in 1198. As to the ancient Doges with whom they are reproached, whatever the *Squittinio della libertà veneta* may say of them, it is evident they were not their Sovereigns.

I shall in all probability be told that the Roman Republic pursued the very retrograde course I have termed impossible, by passing from monarchy to aristocracy, and then to democracy. I cannot agree with those who think they did so.

The first establishment of Romulus was a mixed government, which degenerated soon into despotism. From some particular causes the State perished before its time, as an infant dies before it becomes a man. The expulsion of the Tarquins was the true epoch of the birth of the Republic. But it did not then acquire a consistent form, as the patrician dignity was not abolished, and of course the establishment was only half completed. For that kind of hereditary aristocracy, which is the worst of all legal administration, maintained a continual contest with the democracy, and the form of government never was fixed, as Machiavelli has proved, until the establishment of the tribunes; then only they had a true government, and a real democracy. In fact, the people was then not only the Sovereign, but also the magistrate and judge; and the senate was no more than a subordinate tribunal, for tempering or concentrating the government; while the consuls themselves, although patricians, first magistrates, and generals, and endowed during the time of war with absolute authority, were no more at Rome but presidents of the people.

The government was then soon found to take its natural bent, and to tend strongly towards aristocracy. The patrician rank being abolished, as it were, of itself, the aristocracy was no longer seated in the body of patricians, as it is at Venice and Genoa, but in the body of the senate, composed of patricians and plebeians, and even in the body of tribunes, when they began to assume an active power: for words make no difference in things; and when the people have chiefs who govern for them, under whatever name these chiefs are known, it is always an aristocracy.

The abuse of aristocracy gave birth to the civil wars, and to the Triumvirate. Sulla, Julius Cæsar, and Augustus became in fact real monarchs; and finally, under the despotism of Tiberius, the State was dissolved. Roman history is therefore so far from falsifying my principle that it confirms it. [The *Squittinio* is an anonymous work published in 1612.]

relaxed by enlarging itself, its force is absolutely annihilated, and it can subsist no longer. It is then necessary to gather up and recover its energies, or the State which it sustains will fall into ruin.

The dissolution of the State can happen only in two ways: first, when the prince does not adhere to the laws in the administration of the State and usurps the sovereign power. A very extraordinary change then takes place; the State, not the government, suffers contraction: I mean that the great State is dissolved, and that another is formed from its ruins, composed entirely of the members of the government, who, in their new capacity, bear no other relation to the rest of the people than that of their tyrants and masters. So that the moment the government usurps the sovereignty, the social pact is broken; and all the private citizens, re-entering by right into their natural liberty, are from that time constrained by force, but not obliged by duty, to obey.

The same thing happens when the members of the government usurp separately the power which they ought to exercise only as a body; a circumstance which is no less an infraction of the laws, and occasions even greater disorders. There are then, as it were, as many princes as magistrates, and the State, no less divided than the government, must perish or change its form.

When the State is dissolved, the abuse of government, whatever it is, takes the common name of "anarchy." But, to distinguish, democracy degenerates into "ochlocracy," and aristocracy into "oligarchy"; and I should add, that royalty always changes into "tyranny"; but the term "tyranny" is equivocal, and requires an explanation.

In the vulgar sense of the word, a tyrant is a king who governs with violence and without any regard to justice or the laws. In the exact sense, a tyrant is an individual who arrogates to himself the royal authority without having a right to it. It was to persons of this last description that the Greeks applied the name: they applied it indifferently to good and bad princes whose authority was not lawful.[2] Thus "tyrant" and "usurper" are perfectly synonymous terms.

---

[2] *Omnes enim et habentur et dicuntur tyranni, qui potestate utuntur perpetua in ea civitate quae libertate usa est.* (Cornelius Nepos, *The Life of Miltiades*). ["For all those who hold perpetual power in a State that has known liberty are called and held to be tyrants."] It is true that Aristotle (*Nichomachean Ethics*, Bk. VIII,

That I may apply different names to different things, I shall call the usurper of royal authority a "tyrant," and the usurper of sovereign power a "despot." The tyrant, then, is he who takes upon himself, against the laws, to govern according to the laws; the despot is he who sets himself above even the laws. Thus, the tyrant cannot be a despot, but the despot is always a tyrant.

CHAPTER XI

OF THE DEATH OF THE BODY POLITIC

SUCH IS THE NATURAL and inevitable proneness of the best constituted governments. If Sparta and Rome have perished, what State can expect to last for ever? If we are disposed to form an establishment, let us seek to render it durable, but never hope to make it eternal. Those who would succeed in any undertaking must not attempt impossibilities or flatter themselves that they can give that permanence to the works of man which human things are incapable of.

The body politic, as well as the human body, begins to die from its birth, and bears within itself the causes of its destruction. But the term of existence in both will be longer or shorter, according to the strength or weakness of the constitution. The constitution of man is the work of nature; that of the State is the product of art. Though it does not, consequently, depend on man to ensure himself a long life, it depends on him to give the longest possible existence to a State, by giving it the best possible constitution. Sooner or later, the most vigorous must decay, but it will sink under the hand of time later than any other, unless some unforeseen accident should occur to precipitate its ruin.

The principle of political life is seated in the sovereign authority. The legislative power is the heart of the State, and the executive power

chap. 10) distinguishes the tyrant from the king; the former, he says, reigns only to serve himself, the latter only to serve his subjects. But the Greek authors in general have used the word tyrant in another sense, as appears particularly in the *Hiero* of Xenophon; and, indeed, from Aristotle's distinction we must conclude there has not existed a single king from the commencement of the world.

is the brain which gives motion to all the parts. The brain may become paralytic, and the individual retain life. A man may remain an imbecile and live; but when the heart ceases to perform its functions, the animal is dead.

It is not by the laws that the State subsists, but by the legislative power. The law of yesterday does not hold force to-day; but tacit consent is inferred from silence, and the Sovereign, since it is able to abrogate laws, is deemed to confirm continually whatever laws it does not abrogate. Whatever it has once declared to be its will it wills always, at least until it revokes its declaration.

Why then is so much respect paid to old laws? For the very reason I have just mentioned. It is believed that nothing but the excellency of the wills of those who went before us could have so long preserved them in force; if the Sovereign had not always found them salutary, they would have been undoubtedly revoked. This is the principle upon which the laws in every well-constituted State, so far from weakening, acquire new force continually; our respect for antiquity makes them every day more venerable: whenever the laws are enfeebled by age, we may be assured that the legislative power can no longer exercise its functions, and that the State has expired.

CHAPTER XII

How the Sovereign Authority is Maintained

The sovereign, having no other force but the legislative power, acts only by the laws; and the laws being only the authentic acts of the general will, the Sovereign can never act but when the people are assembled. Some will perhaps think that the idea of the people assembling is a mere chimera. But if it is a chimera now, it was not so two thousand years ago. Have men changed their nature?

The limits of possibility, in moral things, are not so confined as many are apt to suppose them: it is our weakness, our vice, and our prejudice, that narrow the circle. Abject spirits do not believe in great men; and vile slaves reply with a sneer of contempt when we talk of liberty.

By what has been done we may judge what may again be accomplished. I shall not speak of the ancient Grecian Republic; but the Roman Republic I conclude to have been a very great State, and the city of Rome a very large city. By the last census there appeared to be in Rome four hundred thousand citizens that bore arms, and the last time the inhabitants of the Empire were counted, there were found to be above four millions of citizens, without including subjects, foreigners, women, children, or slaves.

What difficulty should we conclude there must be in frequently assembling the immense multitude of this capital and its environs! And yet there passed few weeks without the people of Rome being assembled, and they sometimes met several times in a week. They not only exercised the rights of sovereignty but some part of those of government. They considered certain affairs, they judged certain cases, and came almost as often to the public assembly in the character of magistrates as in that of citizens.

If we recur to the more remote ages, we shall find that the greater part of the ancient governments, even monarchical ones, such as those of the Macedonians and the Franks, had the same councils. Whatever the case, this one incontestable fact answers all difficulties: for to infer what is possible from what has happened seems to me to be good reasoning.

CHAPTER XIII

How the Sovereign Authority is Maintained — *Continued*

It is not sufficient for an assembly of the people to have once fixed the constitution of the State by sanctioning a body of laws, it is not enough that they should have established a perpetual government, or have provided rules, once for all, for the election of magistrates. In addition to extraordinary assemblies which unforeseen events can require, there must be regular and periodic assemblies which nothing can abolish or prorogue, so that on the stated day the people shall be legally convoked, without anything else being needed for their formal convocation,

But, apart from these assemblies which are authorized by their date alone, all assemblies of the people which shall not have been convoked by the magistrates appointed for that purpose, and according to the prescribed forms, must be considered illegal, and the acts of such an assembly can be of no effect, because the very order for assembling must issue from the law.

With respect to the frequency or infrequency of these legal meetings of the people, they must depend on so many considerations that it would be impossible to determine precise rules for them. It can only be said in general that the more powerful the government is, the more frequently the Sovereign ought to show itself.

This, I shall be told, may be good for a single city; but how is it practicable in a State which consists of several cities? Would I, in that case, divide the sovereign authority? Or would I concentrate it in one single city to which all the others must be subject?

I reply that neither one nor the other should be done. In the first place, the sovereign authority is simple and stands alone, and cannot be divided without being destroyed. Secondly, no city, any more than a nation, can be justifiably subjected to another, because the essence of the body politic consists in the union of obedience and liberty, and because the words "subject" and "Sovereign" are the identical correlatives whose meaning is united in the single word "citizen."

I would answer still further that it is always wrong to unite many towns in one city and that whoever makes such a union must not hope to avoid the inconveniences natural to the act. It would be absurd to speak of the abuses prevalent in great States to those who would wish to form only small ones; but how can sufficient force be communicated to little States to defend them from the attacks of great ones, even as the Grecian cities, which once resisted the power of a mighty king, and Holland and Switzerland, which more recently resisted the House of Austria?

Nevertheless, if it is impossible to reduce the State within proper limits, there is still one measure that can be adopted — that of not allowing a capital, but moving the seat of government in rotation to every city, and of assembling by turn in each province of the country.

Let every part of the territory be peopled equally, let the same rights be extended to all, and spread abundance and life through every quarter; by these means the State will become in time the strongest and the best governed that the nature of things will admit of. Remember, likewise, that the walls raised in towns are built upon the ruins of the houses which once ornamented the fields. For every palace I see raised in the capital, I seem to see a whole country desolated.

CHAPTER XIV

How the Sovereign Authority is Maintained — *Continued*

AT THE MOMENT that the people are legally assembled as a sovereign body, all the jurisdiction of government ceases, the executive power is suspended, and the person of the least citizen is as sacred as that of the highest magistrate, because where the person represented may be found, there is no longer a need for a representative. Most of the tumults which happened in the *comitia* at Rome were owing to their being unacquainted with, or at least neglecting, this rule. The consuls were then only the presidents of the people; the tribunes simple speakers,[1] and the senate was absolutely nothing.

These intervals of suspension, when the prince acknowledges, or ought to acknowledge, an actual superior, have always been formidable to that power; and these assemblies of the people, who are the shield of the body politic and the bridle of the government, have ever been the terror of the chiefs, who have spared neither pains nor promises, and have raised every possible objection and impediment, to prevent the citizens from meeting. When the latter are avaricious, pusillanimous, and base, and are more desirous of repose than liberty, they cannot long withstand the redoubled efforts of the government: and thus, the resisting force augments ceaselessly, the sovereign authority vanishes in the end, and most cities fall and perish by a premature fate.

But between the sovereign authority and an arbitrary government there is sometimes an intermediary power introduced, which it is necessary to mention.

[1] The word "Speaker" is used here in nearly the same sense the English Parliament affix to it. The resemblance in these functions would have occasioned conflict between the consuls and the tribunes, even if all jurisdiction had been suspended.

CHAPTER XV

Of Deputies or Representatives

As soon as men cease to consider public service as the principal duty of citizens, and rather choose to serve with their purse than with their persons, we may pronounce the State to be on the very verge of ruin. Are the citizens called upon to march out to war? They pay soldiers for the purpose, and remain at home. Are they summoned to council? They nominate deputies, and stay at home. And thus, in consequence of idleness and money, they have soldiers to enslave their country, and representatives to sell it.

It is the hurry of commerce and of the arts, it is the greedy thirst of gain, and the effeminate softness and love of comfort, that occasion this commutation of money for personal service. Men give up a part of the profits they acquire in order to purchase leisure to augment them. Give money, and you will soon have chains. The word "finance" is a term of slavery; it is unknown in the true city. In a State truly free, the citizens do all with their own arms and nothing with their money; and, instead of purchasing exemption from their duty, they would even pay for fulfilling it themselves. My ideas on this subject are indeed very different from those commonly received; I even think the *corvées*[1] are less an infringement upon liberty than taxes.

The better a State is constituted, the more do public affairs intrude upon private affairs in the minds of the citizens. Private concerns even become considerably fewer, because each individual shares so largely in the common happiness that he has not so much occasion to seek for it in private resources. In a well-conducted city, each member flies with joy to the assemblies; under a bad government, no one is disposed to bend his way thither, because no one is interested in proceedings where he foresees that the general will will not prevail, and in the end every man turns his attention to his own domestic affairs. Good laws lead on to better, and bad ones seldom fail to generate still worse. When once you hear some one say, when speaking of the affairs of the State, "What is it to me?" you may give over the State for lost.

It was the decline of patriotism, the activity of private interest,

[1] [The system of forced labour.]

the immense extent of States, the increase of conquests, and the abuses of government, that suggested the expedient of having deputies or representatives of the people in the assemblies of the nation. These representatives are the body to which, in certain countries, they have dared to give the name of the "Third Estate," as if the private interest of the two other orders deserved the first and second rank, and the public interest should be considered only in the third place.

Sovereignty cannot be represented for the same reason that it cannot be alienated; its essence is the general will, and that will must speak for itself, or it does not exist: it is either itself or not itself: there is no intermediate possibility. The deputies of the people, therefore, are not and cannot be their representatives; they can only be their commissioners, and as such are not qualified to conclude anything definitively. No act of theirs can be a law, unless it has been ratified by the people in person; and without that ratification nothing is a law. The people of England deceive themselves when they fancy they are free; they are so, in fact, only during the election of members of parliament: for, as soon as a new one is elected, they are again in chains, and are nothing. And thus, by the use they make of their brief moments of liberty, they deserve to lose it.

The idea of representatives is modern, and derives its origin from the feudal government, a system absurd and iniquitous, that degrades human nature and dishonours the name of man. The people never had representatives in the republics, nor even in the monarchies, of ancient times; and the word was not known among them. It is very singular that at Rome, where the tribunes were so revered, it was never pretended that they could take upon themselves the functions of the people, and that, in the midst of such a multitude, they never attempted to pass a single *plebiscitum* on their own authority alone. We may judge, however, how embarrassing the great number of people must have been sometimes by what happened in the time of the Gracchi, when some of the citizens were obliged to give their votes from the roofs of the houses.

Where right and liberty fill the minds of men, little regard is paid to any inconveniency that may occur. This was the case with the wise Romans, who gave everything its just due: they permitted the exercise of certain rights to their lictors which their tribunes would not have dared to exert, because there was no danger that the former should ever presume to represent them.

It is true the tribunes did, in certain instances, represent the people; and, in order to explain how they represented them, we must imagine how the government represents the Sovereign. Law being only the declaration of the general will, it is clear that the people cannot be represented in their legislative capacity; but they can, and should be, in the executive power, which is only the force applied to enforce the law. From this we perceive, on examining into the true state of things, that very few nations have any laws. But, with respect to the tribunes, it is certain that no part of the executive power pertained to them, nor could they represent the people of Rome in consequence of the rights annexed to their offices; they could only do so by usurping those of the senate.

Among the Greeks, whatever the people had to do, they did personally, and were continually assembled in the public square.

This they were enabled to be by the mildness of their climate, their exemption from the vice of avarice, and their having a sufficient number of slaves to do their work for them — their important business was liberty. But how can those people who do not enjoy the same advantages exercise the same rights? In your rougher climates you have more wants.[2] Six months of the year the weather will not permit men to remain in the public squares; your dull languages cannot be understood in the open air; you pay more regard to your private gains than to the preservation of your liberty, and are more afraid of becoming poor than of being enslaved.

What! Liberty depend on the servitude of slaves for its support? It is not impossible. The two extremes may act upon each other. Everything that is not in the course of nature has its attendant inconveniences, and civil society most of all. There are situations so peculiarly unfortunate that the liberty of some men cannot be secured but at the expense of the freedom of others, and where the citizen can only be absolutely free by his slave being absolutely subjugated. Such was the situation of Sparta. But as for you, you people of the present day, though you have no slaves, you are yourselves enslaved;

[2] By adopting in cold countries the luxury and effeminate softness of the Orientals, we are sure to adopt their chains; indeed, the one submits us to the other more necessarily than it does them.

you purchase their liberty by the sacrifice of your own. Forbear then to exult in a preference which shows, in my opinion, more baseness than humanity.

I mean not to argue by this that there is a necessity for having slaves, or that the right of slavery is justifiable: so far from it, that I have already proved the contrary. I only explain the reason why the moderns, who believe themselves free, have representatives, and why the ancients had them not. Be the matter of slavery as it will, the moment that a people resign their power into the hands of representatives they are no longer free; they cease to exist.

After having thoroughly investigated the subject, I do not see how it is possible for the Sovereign to preserve henceforth among us the exercise of its rights, unless the city be extremely small. But if it be extremely small will it not be subdued? No. I shall explain presently[3] how the external power of a great people, and the convenient polity and good order of a small State may be united.

CHAPTER XVI

THAT THE INSTITUTION OF GOVERNMENT IS NOT A CONTRACT

THE LEGISLATIVE POWER being once well established, the next point is to establish the executive power; for the latter, whose operations are confined to particular acts, as not sharing the essence of the legislature, is naturally separate from it. If it were possible that the Sovereign, considered as such, could exercise the executive power, right and fact would be so confounded that there would be no means of distinguishing what was or was not law; and the body politic, its nature thus distorted, would soon become the prey to that violence which it was instituted to suppress.

The citizens being all equal by the social contract, whatever all should do, all may prescribe, though no one has a right to require another to do what he does not do himself. And it is properly this right, so indispensable to the life and motion of the body politic, that

[3] This was the object that I had proposed to myself in the sequel to this work; when, in treating of external relations, I came to the confederations which must combine them all. This subject is entirely new, and the principles of it are not yet established.

the Sovereign-delegates to the prince at the institution of government.

Some have pretended that the act of this establishment is a contract between the people and the chiefs they choose for themselves, and that this contract stipulates between the two parties the conditions on which the one is obliged to command and the other to obey. It will be admitted, I am sure, that this would be a strange manner of contracting. But let us see how this opinion is supported.

In the first place, we know that the supreme authority can neither modify nor alienate itself; to limit it would be to destroy it. It is therefore absurd and contradictory to suppose that the Sovereign should give itself a superior; in obliging itself to obey a master, it returns to full liberty.

Besides, it is evident that a contract made between the people and such and such particular persons would be a private act; from whence it follows that this contract could not be a law or an act of sovereignty, and that in consequence it could not be legal.

We see further that the contracting parties, in relation to each other, would be under the law of nature only, and without any guarantee of their reciprocally performing their engagements, a circumstance repugnant in every way to the civil state: as the party which is armed with power is always able to control execution, it is just as inconsistent to suppose the act in question a contract as to suppose that one man contracted with another when he said to him, "I give you all my property, on condition of your returning me just as much as you please of it."

There is but one contract in the State, I mean that of association: all others are excluded by it. No public contract could be imagined which would not be a violation of the first.

CHAPTER XVII

OF THE INSTITUTION OF GOVERNMENT

OF WHAT DESCRIPTION then must we deem the act by which government is instituted? I shall remark, in the first place, that this act is complex, or composed of two others: the establishment of the law, and the execution of the law.

By the first, the Sovereign enacts that there shall be a body of government established under such or such a form; and it is clear that this act is a law.

By the second, the people name the chiefs who shall be charged with the government thus established. But this nomination, being a particular act, is not a second law, but only a consequence of the first and a function of government.

The difficulty here is to understand how there can be an act of government before government exists, and how the people who are but sovereign or subject can become prince or magistrate on certain occasions.

Here we discover one of the astonishing properties of the body politic, by which it reconciles operations so apparently contradictory; for in this act sovereignty is suddenly transformed into democracy in such a manner that, without any sensible change, and merely by a new relation of all with all, the citizens become magistrates, pass from general acts to particular acts, and from making law to the execution of it.

This change of relative situation is not a speculative subtlety of which there is no example in practice: every day in the English Parliament, the House of Commons resolves itself on certain occasions into Grand Committee, for the better discussion of affairs, and becomes a simple commission of that very sovereign court which it formed but the moment before; in this character of a committee, it afterwards reports its proceedings to itself as the House of Commons, and deliberates anew, under another title, on what it has resolved on as a committee.

Such is the advantage peculiar to a democratic government, that it can be established in fact by a simple act of the general will. Subsequently, this provisional government remains in power, if this is the form adopted, or establishes in the name of the Sovereign the government prescribed by law; and the whole proceeding is according to the regulation determined on. It is not possible to institute a legal government in any other manner, or without violating the principles heretofore established.

CHAPTER XVIII

THE MEANS OF PREVENTING THE USURPATIONS OF GOVERNMENT

THE RESULT of these explanations confirms my assertion in the sixteenth chapter that the act which institutes government is not a contract but a law; that the depositaries of the executive power are not the masters of the people but their officers; that the people can establish and remove them when they please; that for them it is not a question of contract but of obedience; and that, in discharging the functions imposed upon them by the State, the members of the executive body only fulfil their duty as citizens, without having any right to dispute about the conditions.

When it happens, therefore, that the people establish an hereditary government, whether it be monarchical, in one family, or aristocratical, in one order of citizens, it is not an engagement which they make: it is a provisional form given to the administration until it shall please the people to order otherwise.

It is true that such changes are always dangerous, and that the established government should never be touched, except when it becomes incompatible with the public welfare; but this circumspection is a maxim of policy, and not a rule of right, and the State is no more obliged to continue civil authority in the hands of its chiefs than military authority in those of its generals.

In proceedings of this nature, it is impossible to observe too carefully all the requisite formalities for distinguishing between a regular and legal act and a seditious tumult, and between the will of all the people and the clamours of a faction. Here above all, when the latter is found to have any influence, the executive power ought not to yield further than is absolutely and strictly required by law; and this obligation gives great opportunity for the prince to maintain his power in spite of the people, and yet avoid the appearance of usurpation; for under colour of only exerting his rights to their full extent, he may easily go beyond the line and, pretending to have the public tranquillity alone in view, prevent the meeting of those assemblies intended for the re-establishment of good order. The silence which the people may be thus compelled to observe, and the excesses which government may at the same time encourage, may become powerful instruments for furthering the schemes of despotism: the former may be urged as a proof that the people approve the conduct of administration, because they fear to complain of it; and the latter employed as a means of drawing punishment on those who have ventured to speak too freely. It was by such kind of practices that the *decemvirs*, who by the laws of their institution were to be elected annually, got their term extended to another year, and in that interval, by preventing the assembling of the *comitia*, they endeavoured to perpetuate their power. The same ready means are employed by all the governments in the world, who, when once they are armed with the public force, are sure to usurp, sooner or later, the sovereign authority.

The periodical assemblies of which I have already spoken are the most proper means to prevent, or at least retard, this evil, above all when they do not need to be formally convened; for in that case the prince cannot prevent their meeting without openly declaring himself a violator of the laws and an enemy of the State.

At the opening of these assemblies, whose only object is the maintenance of the social treaty, two questions should always be proposed, and never on any account omitted, and the votes should be taken separately on each.

The first should be: "Does it please the Sovereign to preserve the present form of government?"

And the second: "Does it please the people to leave the administration with those who are at present charged with it?"

I here presume what I think I have fully demonstrated — namely, that there is not in the State any one fundamental law which cannot be revoked, not even the social compact; because if all the citizens should assemble with one common accord for that purpose, there can be no doubt but it would be legally broken. Grotius thinks that even each citizen can renounce the State of which he is a member,[1] and, resuming his natural liberty and his property, withdraw himself from the country.[2] It would be absurd to suppose that all the citizens united in assembly could not do that which might be done by each of them separately.

[1] [*Op. cit.*, Bk. II, chap. 5.]

[2] But this renunciation must not be made, and the renouncer withdraw, in order to elude his duty, or escape serving his country at the moment it has occasion for his service. His flight then would be a criminal act and punishable as such: it would not be retreat but desertion.

BOOK IV

CHAPTER I

THAT THE GENERAL WILL CANNOT BE DESTROYED

SO LONG AS several men unite and consider themselves as one body, they have but one will, which is to promote the common safety and general well-being. While this union continues, all the springs of the State will be vigorous and simple, the maxims by which they are regulated will be clear and comprehensible; and there will be no jarring, opposing interests; the common good will then be everywhere evident, and nothing will be necessary but a sound understanding to perceive it. For peace, union, and equality are enemies of political subtleties. Men of integrity and simplicity are difficult to deceive because of their very simplicity: lures and refined pretexts do not impose upon them, and they have not even cunning enough to be dupes. When we see, among the happiest people in the world, groups of peasants directing affairs of State under an oak, and always acting wisely, can we help but despise the refinements of those nations which render themselves illustrious and miserable by so much art and mystery?

A State thus governed requires but very few laws; and whenever it becomes necessary to promulgate new ones, the necessity is perceived universally. He who proposes them only says what all have already felt, and neither faction nor eloquence is required to obtain the passage of a measure which each person has already resolved to adopt, as soon as he is sure that the others will act with him.

What leads our reasoners astray on this point is that they consider only those States which have been ill-constructed originally, and suppose, because it would be impossible to pursue in them the system of simple policy I recommend, that it must be equally impossible everywhere. They make great game of the fact that in London or Paris an artful impostor or a man of insinuating eloquence can persuade the people to believe the most ridiculous absurdities. They do not know that Cromwell would be hooted at by the people of Berne, and the

Duke of Beaufort would experience at the hands of the Genevese a discipline he might not greatly admire.

But when the social bond once begins to relax and the State to grow weak, when private interests begin to take the lead, and smaller societies have an influence on the greater, the common interest changes and finds many opposers: there is no longer unanimity of opinion; the general will is no longer the will of all; everything is contested; and the best advice is never adopted without much dispute and opposition.

Finally, when a State upon the brink of ruin supports only a vain illusory form and the social bond no longer unites the hearts of the people, and when the sacred name of public good is made use of to cover the basest interest, then the general will is silenced; and every one, being directed by secret motives, no more gives an opinion as a citizen than if the State had never existed; decrees which have no other object but private interest are then passed, to which the name of laws is falsely given.

But does it follow that the general will is annihilated or corrupted? No: it will remain always constant, unalterable, and pure; but it is rendered subordinate to other wills, which domineer over it. In this state of affairs, though each individual detaches his interest from the common interest, yet he finds it impossible to separate them entirely; but his part of the common ill appears trifling to him when balanced against some private advantage which he has in view. This particular object only excepted, he is in every point as solicitous as any other member to promote the general welfare on his own account. Even by selling his vote for money he does not destroy his own general will, he only eludes it. The fault which such a man commits is that of changing the state of the question, and answering something else than what he was asked: instead of saying by his vote, "It is advantageous to the State," he says, "It is advantageous to such a man, or to such a party, that such a motion should pass." Thus the law for regulating public assemblies is not so much intended to maintain there the general will as to enforce the full and clear repetition of the question on which that will is to determine.

I could make many reflections on the simple right of voting in all acts of sovereignty — a right which nothing can deprive the citizens of; and also upon that of stating opinions, proposing, dividing and discussing, which government is always particularly careful to confine solely to the members of its own body; but this important subject requires a separate treatise, as it cannot be comprehended in that I am now writing.

CHAPTER II

OF SUFFRAGE

IT IS EVIDENT from what has been said in the preceding chapter that the manner of conducting general affairs is the best criterion by which to judge of the morality and health of the body politic. In proportion to the degree of concord which reigns in the assemblies, that is, the nearer opinion approaches unanimity, the more the general will predominates; while tumults, dissensions, and long debates declare the ascendancy of private interests and the declining situation of the State.

This appears less evident when two or more orders enter into the constitution, as the patricians and the plebeians did in Rome, where even in the most glorious days of the Republic, their quarrels frequently disturbed the *comitia*. But this is rather a seeming than a real exception; for there were, by an inherent vice in the body politic, two States, as it were, in one: and what is not true of the two together is true of each one separately. And in fact, even in the most tumultuous times, the *plebiscita* of the people were always tranquil, and there was always a great majority of suffrages when the senate did not mix with them: the citizens having but one interest, the people had but one will.

At the other extremity of the circle, unanimity returns: the citizens are then so sunk in servitude that they have neither liberty nor will. Fear and flattery then make them change their votes into acclamations; instead of deliberating, they adore or they curse. Such was the infamous manner of voting in the senate under the emperors where these acclamations were sometimes made with ridiculous precaution. Tacitus tells us,[1] for instance, that, in the reign of Otho, the senators loaded Vitellius with execrations, and at the same time made a tumultuous noise to prevent him from knowing — lest he should afterwards become their master — what each person had said against him.

[1] [*History*, I, 85.]

From these various considerations, maxims may be drawn for regulating the manner of counting the votes and determining the opinion of a public assembly, which must vary according as the general will is more or less easy to ascertain and the State more or less in decline.

There is one law only which, by its nature, requires unanimous consent; I mean the social compact: for civil association is the most voluntary of all acts; every man being born free and master of himself, no person can under any pretense whatever subject him without his consent. To affirm that the son of a slave is born a slave is to pronounce that he is not born a man.

Should there be any men who oppose the social compact, their opposition will not invalidate it, but only hinder their being included: they are foreigners among citizens. When the State is instituted, residence constitutes consent; to inhabit a territory is to submit to the sovereignty.[2]

Except in this original contract, a majority of votes is sufficient to bind all the others. This is a consequence of the contract itself. But it may be asked how a man can be free and yet forced to conform to the will of others. How are the opposers free when they are in submission to laws to which they have never consented?

I answer that the question is not fairly stated. The citizen consents to all the laws, to those which are passed in spite of his opposition, and even to those which sentence him to punishment if he violates any one of them. The constant will of all the members of the State is the general will; it is by that they are citizens and free.[3] When any law is proposed in the assembly of the people, the question is not precisely to enquire whether they approve the proposition or reject it, but if it is conformable or not to the general will, which is their will. Each citizen, in giving his suffrage, states his mind on that question; and

[2] This must always be understood of a man in a free State; because elsewhere his family, his property, or the want of an asylum to fly to, and also necessity or force, may detain an inhabitant against his will; and then his sojourn does not suppose his consent, either to the contract or to the violation of the contract.

[3] At Genoa we see inscribed over the gates of their prisons and on the chains affixed to their galley slaves the word "Libertas." This application of it is noble as well as just. In fact, it is only the bad people in every State that hinder the citizens from being free. Any country where all such men were chained to the oar would be the seat of perfect liberty.

the general will is found by counting the votes. When, therefore, the motion which I opposed carries, it only proves to me that I was mistaken, and that what I believed to be the general will was not so. If my particular opinion had prevailed, I should have done what I was not willing to do, and, consequently, I should not have been in a state of freedom.

This is indeed supposing that all the characteristics which mark the general will still reside in the most votes: when that ceases to be the case, whatever measures may be adopted, it means the end of liberty.

In showing heretofore how private wills are often substituted for the general will in public deliberations, I have shown the most practicable means of preventing that abuse; and I shall speak again upon the subject later on. With regard to the proportional number of votes necessary to declare this will, I have also laid down the principles on which it should be determined. I have now to add that, though the difference of one single vote will destroy equality, and one opposing voice prevent unanimity, yet there are several grades of unequal division between equality and unanimity, and in each of them the number may be fixed according to the situation and occasions of the body politic.

Two general rules may suffice for regulating these proportions: one is that the more serious and important the deliberations are, the nearer the number of votes which pass them should approach unanimity; the other is that the greater necessity there is for expediting the affair, the smaller may be the majority: and on motions which require to be determined on the spot, a majority of one may be deemed sufficient. The first of these maxims seems most applicable to laws, and the second to practical business. Be that as it may, it is by combining these two rules that the number of voices proper to form the majority on different occasions must be established.

CHAPTER III

Of Elections

WITH REGARD to the elections of the prince and the magistrates, which are, as I have before observed, acts of a complex nature, there are two ways of proceeding in them: the one is by choice, and the

other by lot. Both have been used in various republics, and we see them at this day mixed in a very complicated manner in the election of the Doge of Venice.

"Election by lot," says Montesquieu, "is of the nature of democracy."[1] I grant it is so; but how? "The lot", continues he, "is a form of election that injures no one, but leaves to each citizen a reasonable hope of serving his country." But these are not the reasons.

If we consider that the election of chiefs is one of the functions of government, and not of sovereignty, we shall perceive why the mode of choosing them by lot is more natural to a democracy, where the administration is so much better as its acts are less multiplied.

In all true democracies the office of a magistrate is so far from being advantageous that it is a very burdensome charge, which cannot justly be imposed on one individual rather than on another. The law alone can impose the charge on the person upon whom the lot falls. For the chance being equal for all, and the choice independent of any human will, there is not that application of an act to any particular person which would alter the universality of the law.

In aristocracy, the prince chooses the prince and, the government being preserved by itself, the mode of election by votes is particularly proper there.

The example of the election of the Doge of Venice confirms, instead of destroying, the propriety of this distinction: the mixed form which prevails there agrees with a mixed government. For it is a mistake to suppose the government of Venice to be a true aristocracy. If the people have no part in the government, their nobility is itself the people. A multitude of poor Barnabotes never approach the magistracy, and have nothing belonging to their rank but the empty title of Excellency, and a right of sitting in the Grand Council. This Grand Council being as numerous as our General Council at Geneva, its illustrious members enjoy no more privileges than our plain citizens. It is certain that, allowing for the extreme disparity of the two republics, the burgesses of Geneva exactly represent the Venetian patricians, while our natives and inhabitants may be compared to the townsmen and people of Venice, and our peasants to their subjects on the mainland. In short, in whatever point of view we consider this republic, it will not be found — when allowance is made for its superior great-

[1] [*The Spirit of the Laws*, Bk. II, chap. 2.]

ness — that the government is more aristocratic than ours. The only difference is that, as we have no chief who holds his situation for life, we have not like them occasion for election by lot.

Elections by lot would not be attended with any great inconveniency in a true democracy, where, all being equal in manners and morals, talents, principles, and fortune, it would be indifferent on whom the choice should fall. But I have already said there is not a real democracy existing.

When the two forms of election, that by vote and that by lot, are mixed, the first should be used to fill places which require men of special talents, such as military offices; the other, when good sense, justice, and integrity are sufficient, as they are in judicial offices; for in a well-constituted State these qualities are common to all the citizens.

Neither the choice by lot nor by vote has any place in monarchical government. The monarch being by right the sole prince and magistrate, the choice of his lieutenants pertains to him alone. When the Abbé de Saint-Pierre proposed to multiply the Councils of the King of France and to elect the members by ballot, he perceived not that he was proposing a change in the form of government.[2]

It now remains for me to speak of the manner of giving and collecting votes in the assembly of the people; but perhaps an account of the practice at Rome in this regard will explain it better than all that I could say on the subject. It may not be unworthy the attention of a judicious reader to observe in some detail how both public and private affairs were conducted in a Council of two hundred thousand men.

CHAPTER IV

Of the Roman Comitia

WE HAVE NO authentic records of the earlier ages of Rome; it even appears very probable that most of the accounts transmitted to us of that very remote period are fables,[1] and that part of their annals which

---

[2] [The Abbé de Saint-Pierre's *Project for Perpetual Peace* (1713) was abridged by Rousseau.]

[1] The name of "Rome," which tradition pretends to be derived from Romulus, is a Greek word, and signifies *force;* the name of "Numa" is also Greek, and signifies

is the most interesting in the history of any people, I mean the account of their institution, is entirely lost to us. Experience makes us acquainted every day with the causes from whence the revolutions of empires proceed: but as there is now no opportunity for a new people to be formed, we can do little more than conjecture how they are formed.

The customs which we find established prove at least that these customs had some origin. Of the traditions which trace these customs to their source, we should regard as most certain those which seem to have most reason on their side, and are supported by the best authorities. These are the principles I have adhered to in my researches to discover how the most free and powerful people in the world exercised its supreme power.

After the foundation of Rome, the republic rose into existence; that is, the army of its founder, composed of Albans, Sabines, and foreigners, was divided into three classes, which took from this division the name of tribes. Each of these tribes was subdivided into ten *curiæ* and each *curia* into *decuriæ*, at the head of which were placed chiefs, called *curiones* and *decuriones*.

Besides these divisions, there was drawn from each tribe a body of one hundred cavaliers or knights, called a "century," from whence it appears that these divisions — not very necessary in a city — were at first only a military institution. But it also seems as if the little city of Rome had an instinct for greatness, and formed at once a political establishment suitable for the capital of the world.

An inconveniency soon arose from this first division. While the tribe of the Albans,[2] and that of the Sabines,[3] continued of their original number, the tribe of foreigners,[4] increased by the multitude that flocked to Rome, soon exceeded both the others. The remedy which Servius applied to this dangerous disproportion was a change in the manner of dividing the people. He abolished the division by races and substituted another by which the people were divided according to the parts of the city occupied by each tribe. Instead of three tribes he made four, each of which inhabited one of the hills of

law. What reason have we therefore to suppose that the two first kings of Rome bore these respective names before they performed the acts which these names so well express?

[2] *Ramnenses.*   [3] *Tatienses.*   [4] *Luceres.*

Rome, and took its name from thence. After thus remedying the existing inequality, Servius took measures against its occurring again; he provided that this division be one not only of places but of persons by prohibiting those who resided in one quarter from removing into another; and this prevented the races from mixing.

He also doubled the three ancient centuries of knights, and added twelve others, but still under the ancient names — a simple and judicious method of distinguishing these bodies of knights from the body of the people, without giving the latter any cause to murmur.

To these four city tribes Servius added fifteen others, called country tribes, because they were formed of the inhabitants of the country, divided into as many cantons. There were afterwards as many new ones added; and the Roman people found themselves at last divided into thirty-five tribes, which was the number they were confined to while the Republic continued.

By this distinction of "city tribes" and "country tribes," an effect was produced which is well worthy of attention, because we have no other example of a similar nature, and because Rome owed to it the preservation of her morality and the increase of her empire. It would be natural to suppose that the city tribes would soon arrogate to themselves the highest power and honours, and try to debase the country tribes by every possible means: the fact was exactly otherwise. The partiality of the first Romans for a rural life is well known. This partiality came from their wise institutor, who united liberty with rustic and military labours, at the same time that he relegated, as it were, to the town the arts, crafts, intrigue, wealth, and slavery.

Thus the most illustrious citizens that Rome could ever boast of resided in the fields and cultivated the ground, and it was there that the Romans went to seek those men who were the supporters of the Republic. This kind of rural life being chosen by the noblest patricians, made it universally respected; and the simple and laborious life of a peasant was so much preferred to the idleness and sloth of the burgess of Rome that he who would have been only a miserable proletarian in the city became, as a labourer in the fields, a respected citizen. "It was not without cause," says Varro, "that our magnanimous ancestors established in the country the nursery of those robust and valiant men who were to defend them in time of war and supply them with subsistence in those of peace." Pliny states positively that the rustic

tribes were revered on account of the men who composed them; while
the tribes of the city were held in such contempt that worthless men
were turned over to them as a mark of ignominy. When Appius
Claudius the Sabine came to establish himself in Rome, his name was,
in addition to the other honours conferred upon him, enrolled in one
of these rustic tribes, which afterwards took the name of his family.
Finally, it was into the city tribes, and never into the rustic ones, that
freed-men[5] were admitted; and though by that admission they became
citizens, there was no instance, during the whole time of the Republic,
of one of these freed-men enjoying any office in the magistracy.

This maxim, though a good one, was pushed so far as to produce in
the end a change, and certainly an abuse, in the political system.

In the first place, the censors, after having for a long time claimed
the right of transferring citizens from one tribe to another in a very
arbitrary manner, permitted the greater part of them to inscribe their
names in whatever tribe they chose; a permission which could not be
of utility, and which destroyed an excellent means of censorship.
Besides, all the great and powerful men inscribing their names in the
country tribes, and the freed-men, who had become citizens, remaining
with the populace in the tribes of the city, the tribes in general had no
longer any fixed place for territory, and became so intermixed with
each other that it was by the registers alone that it could be known
what tribe a man belonged to. By this means the word "tribe" was no
longer applied to a real establishment but to persons, or rather became
almost a chimera.

It likewise frequently happened that the tribes of the city, being on
the spot, often found themselves stronger in the *comitia*, and sold the
State to such men as were base enough to purchase the suffrages of
the wretches who composed them.

With regard to the *curiæ*, the institutor having established ten in
each tribe, all the people of Rome being at that time inclosed within
the walls of the city, found themselves comprised in thirty *curiæ*,
each of which had its temples, its gods, its officers, its priests, and its
festivals called *compitalia*, similar to the *paganalia*, afterwards established by the rustic tribes.

In the new division under Servius, the thirty *curiæ* could not be
divided equally between his four tribes, and he was unwilling to touch

[5] [former slaves.]

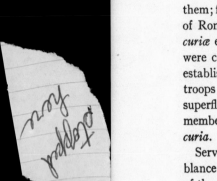

them; from which time they became another division of the inhabitants of Rome, independent of the tribes. But there was no question of *curiæ* either in the rustic tribes or among the people of whom they were comprised, because the tribes, being then considered as a civil establishment entirely, and there having been another mode of raising troops introduced, the military divisions of Romulus were thought superfluous. Thus, though every citizen had his name inscribed as a member of some tribe, there were many who did not belong to a *curia*.

Servius added another division to these two, which bore no resemblance to either of them, and became by its effects the most important of the three. He distributed the entire Roman people into six classes, which were not distinguished by place or by person, but by property, in such a manner that the first classes were filled by the rich, the last by the poor, and the intermediate ones by those who enjoyed moderate fortunes. These six classes were subdivided into one hundred and ninety-three other bodies, called "centuries"; and these bodies were so arranged that the first class alone comprehended more than half of these centuries, and the last class formed only one. Thus the class which contained the fewest men was the most numerous as to centuries, while the entire last class, which alone included more than half the inhabitants of Rome, was counted only as a subdivision.

To prevent the people from foreseeing the consequences of this establishment, Servius affected to give it a military air: he introduced into the second class two centuries of armourers, and two of makers of instruments of war into the fourth. In each class, except the last, he distinguished the young from the old, that is, those who were obliged to bear arms, and those whom the law exempted from that duty on account of their age; a distinction which made it much more necessary than anything relative to property could have done to take a frequent count or census. To complete his plan, he directed the assembly to be held in the Campus Martius, and ordered all who were of an age that subjected them to military service to come to the assembly in arms.

The reason why Servius did not establish this division of young and old in the last class was that the common people, of which it was composed, were not permitted to have the honour of bearing arms for their country; one had to have a hearth to obtain the right to defend it:

and of those innumerable troops of beggars which now glitter in the armies of kings there is perhaps hardly one who would not have been driven with disdain from a Roman cohort at a period when soldiers were the defenders of liberty.

There was, however, a distinction in the last class between the *proletarians*, and those who were called *capite censi*.[6] The first of these, not absolutely destitute of all means, gave citizens to the State, and sometimes soldiers in times of urgent necessity. The latter, who had nothing at all, could only be numbered by their heads, and were considered as nothing. Marius was the first who enrolled any of that body.

Without determining whether this third division was good or evil in itself, I believe I may safely affirm that nothing but the simplicity of manners of the first Romans, their disinterestedness, their taste for agriculture, and their contempt for commerce and wealth, could render this method of classing the people practicable. Where is there a modern people, whose devouring avarice, unquiet spirit of intrigue, continual change of situation, and never ceasing revolutions of fortune would suffer such an establishment to subsist for twenty years without overturning the State? But we must remember that morality and censorship which were stronger than this institution corrected its vices at Rome, and that those rich men who had too much displayed their wealth were exiled into the classes of the poor.

From all this we may easily perceive the reason why we seldom find any more than five classes mentioned, although there were really six. As the sixth furnished neither soldiers for the army nor voters for the Campus Martius,[7] and were hardly of any use in the Republic, they were made little or no account of.

Such were the different divisions of the Roman people. Let us now see the effect which they produced in the assemblies. These assemblies when legally convoked were called *comitia:* they were usually held in the public square in Rome or at the Campus Martius, and were dis-

---

[6] [Traditionally, the Roman census took account of property distinctions; this last class was counted merely as so many heads.]

[7] I say, for the Campus Martius, because it was there that the *comitia* assembled by centuries: in the two other forms, the people assembled at the *forum* or elsewhere; and then the *capite censi* had as much influence and authority as the first citizens.

tinguished by the names of *Comitia Curiata*, *Comitia Centuriata*, and *Comitia Tributa*, according to the form under which they were convoked. The *Comitia Curiata* were instituted by Romulus; the *Comitia Centuriata* by Servius, and the *Comitia Tributa* by the tribunes of the people. No law could be ratified, no magistrate could be elected, but in the *comitia;* and as there was not one citizen whose name did not appear inscribed in some *curia*, century, or tribe, there was of course no citizen excluded from the right of voting. The Roman people were therefore truly sovereign, both in right and in fact.

There were three conditions necessary for making the *comitia* a legal assembly, and stamping the acts there passed with the force of law: first, that the assembly should be convened by a body, or a magistrate, duly authorized by law to convene them; secondly, that the assembly should be held on one of those days permitted by law; and thirdly, that the omens reported by the augurs should be auspicious.

The reason for the first rule requires no explanation. The second was a police regulation: for the holding of the *comitia* was forbidden on those festival or market-days when the country people came to Rome on business, because at such times they did not have time to spend the day at the public meeting. The third served as a kind of check in the hands of the senate to restrain a proud, unquiet people, and temper occasionally the ardour of seditious tribunes; but the latter found more than one means of evading this obstacle.

The laws and the election of chiefs were not the only points submitted to the judgment of the *comitia:* for the people of Rome having usurped the most important functions of government, all the affairs of Europe were in a manner regulated in these assemblies. This diversity of objects obliged the *comitia* to take various forms in these assemblies, according to the business on which it had to pronounce.

To judge properly of these diverse forms, it is enough to compare them. The design of Romulus in instituting the *curiæ* was to restrain the senate by the people, and the people by the senate, while he dominated both equally. He therefore, by this establishment, gave all the authority of number to the people, as a means of balancing the authority of power and wealth which rested with the patricians. But still, according to the spirit of monarchy, he left a great advantage on the patrician side, by the influence which their clients must have on the majority of votes. This admirable institution of patrons and clients was a masterpiece of politics as well as humanity; for without it the patrician order, so adverse to the true republican spirit, could not have been maintained. Rome alone has had the honour of showing the example of this noble institution to the world — an institution from which no evil ever arose, but which has never been followed.

It was from the circumstance of the *curiæ* having persisted under the kings until the time of Servius, and the reign of the later Tarquin not being deemed legal, that the royal laws were generally distinguished by the name of *leges curiatæ*.

In the time of the Republic, the *curiæ* were confined to the four city tribes, and, consequently, consisting only of the populace of Rome, suited neither the senate, which led the patrician order, nor the tribunes; for though these were plebeians, they led those who were in comfortable circumstances. The *curiæ* thus fell into discredit, and their degradation was so extreme at last that thirty lictors used to assemble and do what should have been done by the *Comitia Curiata*.

The division by centuries was so favourable to the aristocracy that it is surprising the senate did not always carry their point in the *comitia* that bore their name, and in which the consuls, censors, and the other curule magistrates were elected. In fact, of the hundred and ninety-three centuries which formed the six classes, containing the whole Roman people, the first class comprehended ninety-eight; and the votes of each class being one for each century, this first class alone had more votes than all the other classes together. Whenever all these centuries voted unanimously on any question, the votes of the centuries of the other classes were not even collected; what the smallest number had decided passed for a decision of the multitude; and it might be said that, in the *Comitia Centuriata*, affairs were regulated by a plurality in money rather than in votes.

But this extreme authority was moderated by a double means. In the first place, the tribunes, as a rule, as well as a great number of plebeians who were in the class of the rich, balanced the credit of the patricians in this first class.

In the second place, instead of having the centuries vote by order of rank, which would have meant always beginning with the first, a regulation was made by which one was chosen by lot, and proceeded alone to the election;[8] and when that was over, the other centuries were called on another day according to their rank, and repeated the same election, and it generally happened that they confirmed its decision. Thus was the authority of example taken away from rank, and made to depend on the lot, a mode more agreeable to the principle of democracy.

There was a further advantage still in this method; for, during the time between the two elections, the country people had leisure to inform themselves concerning the merits of the candidate who had been provisionally nominated, so that they did not have to vote in ignorance. But in time this custom was abolished, under pretence of expediting business, and the two elections were held on the same day.

The *Comitia Tributa* were properly the council of the Roman people. They were convened only by the tribunes. It was in this assembly that the tribunes were elected, and there they passed their *plebiscita*. The senators had not only no rank in the *Comitia Tributa*, but no right even to be present; and being thus forced to submit to laws in the establishing of which they had no vote, the senators were, in this respect, less free than the meanest citizens. This injustice was highly impolitic, and sufficient alone to invalidate the decrees of a body to which all its members were not admitted. If all the patricians had been present at the *comitia*, by virtue of the right they had as citizens, as mere private individuals, they could scarcely have had any influence in decisions where the votes were taken by counting heads, and where the meanest proletarian would have as good a vote as the chief of the senate.

Thus we see that besides the order which was a result of these various methods of counting the votes of so great a people, the various methods were not reducible to forms indifferent in themselves, but that each of them produced effects corresponding to the objects of their institution.

Without entering further into long details, it must appear from the account already given that the *Comitia Tributa* were the most favourable to popular government, and the *Comitia Centuriata* to aristocracy. With regard to the *Comitia Curiata*, where the populace of Rome alone

---

[8] The century thus chosen by lot was called *prærogativa*, as being the first whose suffrage was demanded. From hence comes the word *prerogative*.

formed a majority, as they seemed likely to answer no one purpose but that of favouring tyrants and all kinds of evil designs, they fell into such disrepute that even seditious men avoided going to them, lest it should betray that they had some dark project in contemplation. It is certain that it was in the *Comitia Centuriata* alone that all the majesty of the Roman people was displayed. They alone were complete; for the *Comitia Curiata* excluded the country tribes, and the *Comitia Tributa* the senate and the patricians.

The manner of taking the votes was in the earlier days of Rome as simple as the manners of the inhabitants, although less simple than at Sparta. Every voter gave his vote aloud, and a secretary inscribed it in a register; the majority of votes in each tribe was considered as the vote of the tribe; and the majority of these votes was considered as the vote of the people; and the same rule was observed with respect to the *curiæ* and centuries. This was a judicious mode so long as integrity reigned among the citizens, and each individual was ashamed to give publicly the sanction of his vote to an unjust or unworthy cause; but when the people became corrupt enough to sell their votes, it was necessary that votes should be given in a secret manner in order to restrain the purchasers by mistrust and give the knaves an opportunity not to be traitors.

I know that Cicero condemns this alteration, and attributes to it in part the ruin of the Republic. But though I acknowledge the weight of Cicero's authority here, I cannot agree with his opinion. I think, on the contrary, that the fall of Rome was accelerated by the want of enough such alterations. For as a regimen proper for persons in health will not agree with invalids, so a corrupted people cannot be governed by the same laws that will suit a good people. Nothing can illustrate this maxim more than the state of Venice, whose Republic still continues, or at least the semblance of it, from no other reason than because the laws were adapted for the government of wicked men.

Such were the reasons that tablets were distributed to the citizens, by which each could vote without any one else knowing on what side his vote was given. New forms were also established for collecting these tablets, counting voices, comparing numbers, etc.; but all this did not prevent suspicion of infidelity in the officers employed on these occasions;[9] and the multitude of edicts passed to prevent intrigue and traffic in votes proved how useless they were.

Towards the latter years of the Republic, there was often a necessity for recurring to extraordinary expedients to supplement the deficiency of the laws. Sometimes omens were drawn from supposed prodigies; but this could only impose upon the people, without producing any effect on those who governed them. Sometimes an assembly was convened so hastily that the candidates had no time to carry out their intrigues; and sometimes, when it was perceived that the people were prepared to give their votes to an unworthy cause, the whole time of the meeting was consumed in long harangues. But ambition found means to elude all these schemes; and — what seems almost incredible — in the midst of all these abuses, this immense people, by virtue of their ancient regulations, never desisted from electing their magistrates, passing laws, judging causes, and expediting all affairs, whether of a public or private nature, with almost as much facility as they could have been transacted in the senate itself.

CHAPTER V

OF THE TRIBUNESHIP

WHEN IT IS FOUND impossible to establish an exact proportion between the different parts of the State, or when irremediable causes are continually altering the relations between the parts, then a particular magistrate is created, who does not become one of the body of magistrates, but whose relative affinity to each enables him to form an intermedial degree or link of union between the prince and the people, or between the prince and the Sovereign, or even between both at once, if it be necessary.

This body, which I shall call the "tribuneship," is the means of preserving the laws and the legislative power. They sometimes guard the Sovereign against the government, as the tribunes of the people did at Rome; and sometimes the government against the people, as the Council of Ten now does in Venice; and sometimes they maintain

---

[9] *Custodes, diribitores, rogatores suffragiorum.*

a proper equilibrium between the parts of the State, as the *ephors* did at Sparta.

The tribuneship is not a constituent part of the city, nor can it enjoy any share in the legislative or executive power: but it is in this very fact that its own power is the greater; for, though it can do nothing, it can prevent everything. It is more sacred and more revered as the defender of the laws, than the prince who executes them, or the Sovereign which institutes them. This veneration paid to tribunes was very conspicuous at Rome, where those proud patricians who despised the whole body of the people were obliged to bend before one simple officer of that people, though he possessed neither patronage nor jurisdiction.

The tribuneship, wisely tempered, is the firmest support of a good constitution; yet the conferring upon that office of but a very small degree of power beyond what is absolutely requisite, is the certain means of overturning everything: from the nature of the office of tribune, it can never be feeble; for provided it is something, it is never less than it should be.

This office degenerates into tyranny when it usurps the executive power, which it is designed only to moderate, or when it attempts to dispense with the laws, which it ought to protect. The prodigious power of the *ephors*, though inoffensive while Sparta maintained her morality, accelerated her corruption when once it had commenced. The blood of Agis, assassinated by these tyrants, was avenged by his successor; the crime and the punishment of the *ephors* equally contributed to the fall of the Republic; and after Cleomenes Sparta was no more. Rome fell by the same means; the tribunes there also by degrees usurped excessive power, which, aided by the laws that were made for the support of liberty, they employed to support the emperors who destroyed it. As to the Council of Ten at Venice, it is a tribunal of blood, formidable alike to the patricians and the people, and, so far from protecting the laws with a jealous pride, it serves only, after their debasement, to give those blows in secret which are too black for public view.

The tribuneship, like the government, is weakened by the multiplication of its members. When the tribunes of the Roman people, who were at first only two, but afterwards increased to five, were desirous of doubling their number, the senate gave no opposition, being well assured of what afterwards actually happened; that in such a number they might find some means of playing one against another.

The best means of preventing the usurpations of so formidable a body — but a means which no government seems ever to have considered — would be not to make their establishment permanent, but to fix stated intervals when it should suffer a temporary suppression. These intervals should not be so long as to give time for abuses to become strong, and should be settled by law, with a provision for shortening the time, if necessary, by extraordinary commissions.

This method appears to me wholly unobjectionable, because, as I have already observed, the tribuneship, making no part of the constitution, may be suppressed without doing the constitution any violence; and I am inclined to believe it would be effectual, because a newly restored magistrate does not start with the power which his predecessor might have acquired, but with that bestowed upon him by the law.

CHAPTER VI

OF THE DICTATORSHIP

THE INFLEXIBILITY natural to laws, which hinders their bending to events, may in certain cases be pernicious, and, in a crisis, even occasion the ruin of the State. The order and slowness of legal forms require a space of time which circumstances sometimes refuse. And as there are a thousand occurrences for which the legislator has not provided, it is a very necessary part of foresight to perceive that everything cannot be foreseen.

For this reason it is advisable not to establish political institutions so strongly as to prevent a possibility of suspending their operation. Even Sparta herself suffered her laws to lie dormant.

However, nothing but the greatest dangers ought to weigh against the danger of altering the regular course of public order, and the sacred power of the laws should never be impeded but when the salvation of the country depends upon it. In these rare instances, when the necessity is manifest, the public safety is provided for by a private act,[1] which commits its charge to the most worthy. This commission may be given in two different ways, according to the nature of the danger.

If it is sufficient for a remedy to have the activity of government augmented, then the mode must be to concentrate power in the hands of one or two of its members: by which means it will not be the authority of the laws that is altered, but only the form of administering them. But if the danger is such that the apparatus of the laws is an obstacle to their preservation, then a supreme chief must be appointed, who shall be able to silence the laws and suspend for a moment the sovereign authority. In such a case, the general will is not to be doubted, because it is evident that the first intention of the people must be that the State should not perish. This manner of suspending the legislative authority does not abolish it: the magistrate who silences it cannot make it speak; he dominates it, but he cannot represent it. He can do everything but make laws.

The first of the two modes was the one adopted by the Roman senate when they invested their consuls, by a consecrated formula, with power to save the Republic. The second was employed when one of the two consuls named a dictator, a practice of which Alba had given an example to Rome.[2]

In the infancy of the Republic, they often had recourse to dictatorship, because the State had not then acquired sufficient stability to support itself by the strength of its constitution alone. The morality of the times rendered those precautions then superfluous which would have been necessary at another period; and there was no fear that a dictator would either abuse his authority or endeavour to protract it beyond its term. It seemed, on the contrary, that such abundant power was burdensome to the person on whom it was deposited, and that he made haste to be released from a dangerous and troublesome office which made him stand in the place of the laws.

Thus it is not the danger of its abuse, but the danger of its degradation, that makes me criticize the indiscreet use of this supreme magistracy in the earliest ages. For while that authority was lavished on elections, dedications, and things of mere formality, there was reason

---

[1] [An act with a private object, i.e., to choose a particular individual.]

[2] This nomination was made secretly, and in the night, as if they were ashamed of placing a man above the laws.

to apprehend that it would become less formidable when it was needed, and that the people would at last be accustomed to regard the name of dictator as an empty title, employed only to give dignity to idle ceremonies.

Towards the end of the Republic, the Romans having become more circumspect, the dictatorship was as imprudently withheld as it had been lavishly bestowed in former times. It is easy to see that their fears were ill-founded, that the weakness of the capital was a sufficient security against the magistrates lodged within its bosom; that a dictator might, in certain cases, defend the public liberty, but could never injure it; and that it was not in Rome, but in her armies, that her chains were forged. The little resistance that was made by Marius against Sulla, and by Pompey against Cæsar, clearly showed what could be expected from authority from within against force from outside.

This mistake led the Romans into great errors: for instance, in not appointing a dictator in the conspiracy of Catiline; for it was only a question of the city itself, and at most, of some province in Italy, and the unbounded authority which the laws gave to the dictator would have enabled him easily to dissipate the conspiracy, which was only stifled by a concurrence of fortunate events which human prudence could never have expected.

Instead, the senate contented itself with transmitting all its power to the consuls, which obliged Cicero, in order to give efficacy to his measures, to exceed his power in a very material point; and though, in the first transports of joy, his conduct was approved, it was not without justice that in the end he was called to account for the blood of citizens which was shed in violation of the laws — a reproach which could not have been levelled at a dictator. But the consul's eloquence carried everything before it; and he, although a Roman, being more attached to his own glory than to his country, passed over the more lawful and more certain means of saving the State, that he might have the honour of its protection entirely to himself.[3] Thus he was honoured, and justly, as the liberator of Rome, but he was punished with equal justice as a violator of her laws. However glorious his recall might have been, still it was only an act of grace towards him.

[3] It was this that he could not be sure of, if he proposed a dictator; he did not dare to name himself, and he could not be sure that his colleagues would name him.

In whatever manner this important commission of dictator is conferred, it is important that it should hold in force but a very short time, and that nothing should be allowed to prolong it: for in the crisis which produces it, the State must fall or be saved very speedily; and if the dictatorship remains after the pressing occasion for its establishment is removed, it becomes either tyrannical or useless. At Rome the dictators held office only for six months, and most of them abdicated before the expiration of their term. If the term had been longer, there might have been a temptation to prolong it still further, as was the case with the *decemvirs,* whose office continued for a year. The dictator was possessed of power only just long enough to perform the service for which he was appointed, and had not time to think of forming other projects.

CHAPTER VII

Of the Censorship

In the same manner as the general will is declared by the law, the public judgment is declared by the censorship; public opinion is the kind of law of which the censor is the minister, and which he only causes to be applied to particular cases, after the example of the prince.

The censors are so far from being the arbiters of the people's opinion, that their business is only to declare it, and whenever they cease to do so faithfully, their decisions are vain and of no effect.

It is useless to distinguish the morality of a nation from the objects of its esteem; for both originate in the same principle and are necessarily indistinguishable. Throughout the world, it is not nature but opinion that determines mankind in the choice of its pleasures. When our errors of opinion are corrected, our morality reforms of itself. What is, or what appears to be good, attracts universal admiration; but it is in judging what is good that men make mistakes; so that the great point is to regulate this judgment. Who judges of morality judges of honour; who judges of honour takes his law from opinion. The opinions of a people are born of its constitution; for, though law does not regulate morality, yet legislation gives birth to it; when legislation becomes feeble, morality degenerates: but then the judgment of the censor will not effect what the force of the laws could not accomplish.

The conclusion to be deduced from these remarks is that the censorship may be of utility in preserving morality, but it can never restore it. Censors should be appointed while the laws are in their vigour; for when they have fallen into decay, all is over; nothing justifiable can have force when the laws have lost it.

The business of the censorship is to preserve morality by preventing the opinions of men from being corrupted, to maintain their integrity by judicious aids, and sometimes even to fix opinions when they waver. The use of seconds in duels, which was carried to a pitch of frenzy in the Kingdom of France, was abolished by these words only, in an edict issued by the King: "As for those who have the cowardice to call on seconds." This judgment, by anticipating the public judgment, quickly determined it. But when similar edicts tried to declare it cowardice to fight a duel also, though the assertion was true, yet, as it contradicted the received opinion, the public ridiculed a decision on a matter on which it had already determined its judgment.

I have said, in a former work,[1] that public opinion not being subject to any restraint, no appearance of restriction need exist in a tribunal established to represent it. It is impossible to admire too much the art with which this resource, entirely lost among the moderns, was put to work by the Romans, and even more by the Lacedemonians.

A man of profligate character advised a salutary measure in the Spartan Council, and the *ephors*, without seeming to pay any regard to what he had said, caused a citizen of known integrity to propose the very same measure. How great an honour was conferred by this act upon the one party, and what a severe reproach did it cast upon the other, without making use of either praise or censure in direct terms! At another time, when certain drunken men of Samos[2] had defiled the tribunal of the *ephors* with filth, an edict appeared the next day granting full permission to the Samians to commit filthy

---

[1] I touch but slightly in this chapter on a subject which I have already treated upon more at large in the *Letter to M. d'Alembert*.

[2] They were from another island, which the delicacy of our language forbids me to name on this occasion. [Rousseau is speaking of Chios.]

deeds. A real punishment would have been less severe than such an impunity. When Sparta pronounced what was or was not virtuous, Greece did not appeal from her decisions.

CHAPTER VIII

OF CIVIL RELIGION

IN THE FIRST AGES of the world, men knew no kings but the gods, and no government but theocracy. They reasoned like Caligula, and their reasoning, at that time, was just. It requires the work of a very long period so to alter the sentiments and ideas of mankind as to make them acknowledge their fellow mortals for their masters, and flatter themselves that they will find their advantage in submitting to them.

From this single circumstance of there being a god placed at the head of every political society, it is evident that there were as many gods as peoples. Two peoples, strangers to each other, and almost always in a state of hostility, could not long continue to acknowledge the same master: two armies fighting against one another could not obey the same chief. Thus polytheism was the consequence of national divisions; and polytheism in turn gave rise to civil and religious intolerance, which are the same by nature, as I shall show hereafter.

The propensity which the Greeks indulged of discovering that it was their own deities who were worshipped even by barbarians sprung from that of regarding themselves as the natural sovereigns of those peoples. But in our days it is certainly a very ridiculous species of erudition that revolves around the question of the identity of the gods of different nations: as if Moloch, Saturn, and Chronos could be the same god! As if the Baal of the Phœnicians, the Zeus of the Greeks, and the Jupiter of the Latins could be the same! As if there could be something common to chimerical beings that have different names!

It may appear extraordinary that, in the days of paganism, when each State had its own cult and its own gods, there should have been no religious wars. The reason was that each State, having its peculiar

cult as well as its own form of government, did not distinguish its gods
from its laws. Political war was also theological; the jurisdiction of
their gods being, as it were, limited by the boundaries of the nation.
The gods of one country had no right over the people of another.
The gods of the pagans were certainly not jealous gods; for they divided
the empire of the world among themselves: even Moses and the
Hebrews lent themselves to this idea sometimes in speaking of the
God of Israel. They regarded, it is true, as nothing the gods of the
Canaanites, a people proscribed and condemned to destruction, and
whose country they were to possess; but see how these Hebrews spoke
of the deities of the neighbouring peoples whom they were forbidden
to attack! "The possession of that which appertains to Chamos
your god," said Jephthah to the Ammonites, "is it not lawfully yours?
We possess, under the same title, the lands which our conquering God
has acquired."[1] This seems to me to be fully acknowledging a parity
between the rights of Chamos and those of the God of Israel.

But when the Jews, after being subject to the kings of Babylon
and, later, to those of Syria, obstinately refused to acknowledge any
other god but their own, the refusal was regarded as rebellion against
their conquerors and drew upon them the persecutions which we read
of in their history, and which were unrepeated until the commencement
of Christianity.[2]

Every religion, therefore, being peculiarly united with the laws of
the State which prescribed it, there was no way of converting a people
but by enslaving them, nor were there any other missionaries but
conquerors; and the obligation of exchanging one cult for another
being a law imposed on the vanquished, men had to conquer before
they began to convert. So far indeed were men from fighting for the
gods, that it was the gods, as in Homer, that fought for the men; each
party demanded victory from his own god and repayed him for it by

---

[1] "*Nonne ea quæ possidet Chamos deus tuus, tibi jure debentur?*" (Judges XI, 24)
Such is the text of the Vulgate. Father de Carrières has translated it: "Believe
you not that you have a right to possess that which appertains to Chamos your
god?" I do not know the force of the Hebrew text; but I see that, in the Vulgate,
Jephthah acknowledges the right of the God Chamos unequivocally, and that the
French translator weakens this acknowledgment by an "according to you,"
which is not in the Latin.

[2] It is evident that the Phocian war, which was called "sacred," was not a religious
war. Its object was to punish sacrilege, and not to subdue unbelievers.

additional altars. The Romans, before they took a place, summoned its gods to abandon it; and when they left the Tarentines with their angry deities, it was because they considered these deities as being already subjugated to their own and forced to do them homage. They indeed often left the people they had vanquished their gods, in the same manner that they left them their laws. A wreath presented to the Jupiter of the Capitol was frequently the only tribute they imposed.

Finally, the Romans having extended with their empire both their cult and their gods, and having often adopted those of the conquered by granting to both the right of the city, the peoples of that vast empire insensibly found themselves with a multitude of gods and cults, everywhere almost the same: and that is how paganism became, throughout the known world, one single religion.

While things were in this situation, Jesus came to establish a spiritual kingdom on earth, which, by separating the theological from the political system, made the State no longer one, and caused those intestine dissensions which have never ceased to agitate the Christian peoples. This novel idea of a kingdom of the other world could never have entered the heads of pagans, and they always considered the Christians as really rebels, who, with a hypocritical air of entire submission, were only seeking the opportunity of rendering themselves independent and masters by artfully usurping the authority which in their weakness they pretended to respect. This was the cause of the Christians being persecuted.

What the pagans had feared actually came to pass. The entire face of affairs was altered; the humble Christians changed their language, and soon this pretended kingdom of the other world became, under a visible chief, the most violent despotism in this.

However, as there had always been a prince and civil laws, the consequence resulting from this double power has been a perpetual conflict for jurisdiction which has made any system of good polity impossible in Christian States; and men could never certainly inform themselves whether it was the master or the priest they were bound to obey.

Several peoples, even in Europe and its vicinity, have endeavoured to preserve, or rather re-establish, the ancient system, but without success; the spirit of Christianity prevails over everything. The

sacred cult has always remained or has again become independent of
the Sovereign, and has had no necessary link to the body of the State.
Mahomet evinced very sane views, and linked his political system well
together; and while the form of government established by him subsisted under the caliphs, his successors, it was undivided; and in that
respect it was good. But the Arabs, having become flourishing, learned
and polished, became also luxurious and effeminate, and were subjugated by the barbarians: the division between the two powers then
began again; and although this division is less apparent amongst the
Mahometans than the Christians, it none the less exists, and conspicuously so in the sect of Ali, and in those States, such as Persia,
where it continually makes itself felt.

Among us, the Kings of England are acknowledged heads of the
Church, and the Czars have adopted the same character: but by
this title they are rendered the ministers rather than the masters of
the Church; they have acquired only the right of maintaining it, and
not that of altering it; they are not its "legislators" but only its
"princes." Wherever there is formed a body of the clergy[3] it is master
and legislator in its country. There are therefore two powers, two
Sovereigns, in England and in Russia as well as in other countries.

Of all Christian authors, the philosopher Hobbes is the only one
who has clearly seen the evil and its remedy, and who has dared to
propose a junction of the two heads of the Eagle, and the complete
restoration of political unity, without which no State or government
can ever be well-established.[4] But he ought to have seen that the
dominating spirit of Christianity would defeat his system, and that
the interest of the priesthood would always triumph over that of the
State. It is not so much what is hideous and false in his political
theory, as what is just and true, that has rendered it odious.[5]

[3] It should be observed that it is not so much the formal assemblies of the clergy,
like those in France, which bind them together as the communion of the Churches.
Communion and excommunication are the social compact of the clergy, by means
of which they will always be masters over peoples and kings. All priests who
communicate together, though they dwell in the two extremities of the earth, are
fellow citizens; an invention which may be truly termed a masterpiece of politics.
There was nothing like it among pagan priests, neither did they ever form a body
of clergy.

[4] [Rousseau refers to Hobbes' *De Cive* (1642), which contained the first influential
arguments for the supremacy of secular over ecclesiastical authority.]

[5] In a letter from Grotius to his brother, dated the 11th of April, 1643, it appears

I believe that by developing the historical facts from this point of view, an easy refutation would be given to the very opposite opinions of Bayle[6] and Warburton[7], one of whom pretends that religion is of no use to a body politic, while the other, on the contrary, asserts that Christianity is the only certain support of it. We should prove to the first writer that no State has ever been established without having religion for its basis; and to the other that the Christian law is at bottom more injurious than useful to the constitution of the State. The ideas of many people on religious matters are so exceedingly vague that, to make myself clearly understood, it may be necessary to fix them with a little more precision on those points which relate to my subject.

Religion, considered in its relation to society, which is either general or particular, may also be divided into two distinct species: the religion of man, and the religion of the citizen. The former, without temples, altars, or rites, and confined entirely to the purely internal cult of the supreme God and the eternal duties of morality, is the pure and simple religion of the Gospel, the true theism, and what may be justly called the "natural divine law." The other, set down only for one country, gives it its gods, and its own tutelary patrons; it has its dogmas, its rites, and its external cult prescribed by the law; but if you pass the boundaries where this religion prevails, its followers consider every human being as a stranger, an infidel, a barbarian; they will allow the rights or the duties of man only to those who live in the circle of their own altars. Such were, in the first ages, all the religions to which we may give the name of "civil" or "positive divine law."

There is still a third and more bizarre kind of religion, which gives

how far that learned man approved, and how far he disapproved, of the *De Cive*. It is true that, inclining to the indulgent side, he seems to pardon the good part of the author's doctrine on account of the bad maxims he inculcates; but not every one is so forgiving.

[6] [Pierre Bayle (1647–1706), author of the *Dictionnaire historique et critique*, and *Pensées sur la comète*, and a precursor of the eighteenth-century *philosophes*. In his *Pensées sur la comète*, Bayle argued that "atheism does not necessarily lead to the corruption of morality."]

[7] [Warburton argued, especially in his most famous work, *The Divine Legation of Moses demonstrated on the Principles of a Religious Deist* (1737–41), that religion, and in particular the revealed doctrine of future rewards and punishments, is necessary for the maintenance of morality and civil society.]

to mankind two codes of legislation, two chiefs, and two countries, requires from them contradictory duties, and prevents their being devout men and citizens at the same time. The religion of the Lamas is one of this sort, so is that of the Japanese, and so is Roman Christianity. The last may well be called the religion of the priest. There results from it a kind of mixed and unsocial law which is without a name.

From a political point of view, these three kinds of religion all have their defects. The third in particular is so evidently bad that it would be losing time to demonstrate its evils. Whatever breaks social unity is worthless; all institutions which set man in contradiction with himself are worthless.

The second is good in that it unites the divine cult with love of the laws, and, by making their country the object of the citizens' adoration, it teaches them that to serve the State is to serve its tutelary God. This is a species of theocracy, which allows of no pontiff but the prince, or any priests but the magistrates. To die for one's country is martyrdom; to violate the laws is impiety; and to submit a criminal to public execration is to condemn him to the anger of the gods: *Sacer estod.*

But this religion is also evil, because, as it is founded in error and falsehood, it deceives mankind, renders it credulous and superstitious, and clouds the true worship of the Divinity with vain ceremonies. It is likewise evil, when becoming jealous and tyrannical, it makes a people sanguinary and intolerant to such a degree that they breathe nothing but massacre and murder, and believe they perform a sacred action in killing every person who will not bow to their gods. This places such a people in a state of natural warfare with all other people, and must be extremely injurious to their own safety.

There now remains to be considered the religion of man, or Christianity, not as it is at this day, but such as it is in the Gospel, which is very different. By this religion — holy, sublime, and true — mankind, the children of the same God, acknowledges all the human race as brothers, and the society which unites them dissolves' not even at death.

But this religion, having no particular connection with the body politic, leaves the laws possessed only of that force which they draw from themselves, and does not give them any additional power; and thus one of the great bonds of particular societies is wanting. And what is of still more consequence, this system, instead of attaching the hearts of citizens to the State, draws off their attention from all earthly concerns. I know of nothing more destructive to the social spirit.

It has been said that a nation of true Christians would form the most perfect society that can be conceived. There is only one circumstance which makes me greatly doubt the truth of this supposition: it is that a society of true Christians would not be a society of men.

I say further that such a society, supposing it could exist, would be neither more strong nor more durable for all its perfection: in consequence of its being perfect, it would want the necessary bond of connection; and its very perfection would prove the vice that must destroy it.

Every one would do his duty; the people would be obedient to the laws, the chiefs just and moderate, the magistrates upright and incorruptible; the soldiers would despise death; neither vanity nor luxury would be known: all that is very good; but let us look a little further.

Christianity is a religion entirely spiritual and occupied only with the things of heaven; the country of the Christian is not of this world. It is true, he performs his duty, but it is with perfect indifference as to the good or ill success of his cares. Provided he has nothing to reproach himself with, it is of little consequence in his opinion whether affairs go well or ill here below. If the State flourishes, he scarcely dares to enjoy the public felicity, lest he should become proud of the glory of his country; and if the nation falls into ruin, he blesses the chastening hand of God which is laid so heavily on His people.

For such a society to remain in peace and preserve uninterrupted harmony, all the citizens, without exception, must be equally good Christians: but if there should unhappily be found among them one single man of ambition or one hypocrite, a Catiline, for instance, or a Cromwell, he would make fine work with his pious neighbours. Christian charity does not easily permit men to think ill of their neighbours. When a man, such as I have just named, finds, by some subtle art, the means of imposing on his fellow citizens and of attracting to himself some part of the public authority, the consequence is that he would be a man established in dignity, a man intended by God to be respected: very soon there is a power; God intends it to be obeyed; and if this depository of their whole power should abuse it, it is the rod with which God punishes His children. Men would create moral scruples for themselves about chasing away the usurper: the public repose must be interrupted, violence must be used, and blood shed; all this agrees ill with Christian meekness; and, after all, what does it avail whether we are in freedom or in chains during our pilgrimage through this vale of misery? For Paradise is the happy goal in view, and resignation only an additional means of gaining it.

If the State is engaged in a war with strangers, the citizens march without dread to battle, and not one of them thinks of flight; but, though they do their duty, they have no ambition to be victorious; they know better how to die than how to conquer. What signifies it to us, say they, whether we vanquish or are vanquished? Does not Providence know better than we what is proper for us? It is easy to suppose that a proud, impetuous, and passionate enemy would not fail to take advantage of such pious stoicism! Let us for a moment suppose this meek and patient people engaged in a quarrel with one of those generous peoples, who are devoured by ardent love of glory and of country; suppose this republic of Christians contending with Sparta or with Rome: the pious Christians would be beaten, crushed, destroyed, before they had time to collect themselves; or they must owe their salvation to the contempt of the enemy for them. It was, in my opinion, a fine oath that was taken by the soldiers of Fabius, who did not swear to conquer or die, but swore to come back victorious, and kept their oath. Never would Christians have taken such an oath; they would have thought it was tempting God.

But I am guilty of an error when I speak of a republic of Christians, for each of the terms excludes the other. Christianity preaches only servitude and dependence. Its spirit is too favourable to tyranny not to be always taken advantage of. True Christians are formed to be slaves, and they are so sensible of it that they hardly endeavour to avoid slavery; this short life is of too little consequence in their eyes to have any thought bestowed upon it.

We are told that Christian troops are excellent. I deny it. Where are they to be found? For my part, I do not know of any Christian troops. If I am desired to recollect the Crusades, I shall beg leave to remark, without disputing the bravery of the Crusaders, that, so far from being Christian troops, they were the soldiers of the priests, citizens of the Church who fought for their spiritual country, which by some means or other the Church had rendered temporal. In fact, when we consider the point, this goes back to paganism: as the Gospel does not establish any national religion, all holy wars are impossible among Christians.

Under the pagan emperors, the Christian soldiers were distinguished for their bravery, as the Christian writers assure us; and I believe the fact was so: it was the effect of honourable emulation of the pagan troops. When the emperors became Christians, this spirit of emulation died away; and, as soon as the Cross had chased the Eagle from the field of glory, the valour of the Romans was no more.

But, leaving these political considerations, let us return to the subject of right, and lay down fixed principles on that important point. The right which the social compact gives the Sovereign over the subjects extends no further than is necessary for the public good.[8] No Sovereign can therefore have a right to control the opinions of the subjects any further than as these opinions may effect the community. It is of consequence to the State that each of its citizens should have a religion which will dispose him to love his duties; but the dogmas of that religion interest neither the State nor its members except as far as they affect morality and those duties which he who professes them is required to discharge towards others. For the rest, every individual may entertain what opinions he pleases, without it pertaining to the Sovereign to take cognizance of them; for, having no jurisdiction in the other world, whatever the fate of its subjects in the life to come, it is not the Sovereign's business, provided they are good citizens in the present one.

There is therefore a purely civil profession of faith, the articles of which it is the business of the Sovereign to arrange, not precisely as dogmas of religion, but as sentiments of sociability without which it

[8] "In a republic," says the Marquis d'A. [d'Argenson], "each person is perfectly at liberty to do whatever does not injure others." That is the invariable boundary; and it is impossible to fix it with greater precision. I cannot deny myself the pleasure of quoting this manuscript sometimes, though it is unknown to the public, in order to do honour to an illustrious and respectable man, who, even in the ministry, preserved the heart of a faithful citizen, and just and wholesome ideas on the government of his country. [The Marquis d'Argenson was for a period French Minister of Foreign Affairs.]

is impossible to be either a good citizen or a faithful subject.[9] The Sovereign has no power by which it can oblige men to believe them, but it can banish from the State whoever does not believe them; not as an impious person, but as an unsociable one, who is incapable of sincerely loving the laws and justice, and of sacrificing, if occasion should require it, his life to his duty as a citizen. But if any one, after he has publicly subscribed to these dogmas, shall conduct himself as if he did not believe them, he is to be punished by death. He has committed the greatest of all crimes: he has lied in the face of the law.

The dogmas of civil religion ought to be simple, few in number, precisely fixed, and without explanation or comment. The existence of a powerful, wise, and benevolent Divinity, who foresees and provides the life to come, the happiness of the just, the punishment of the wicked, the sanctity of the social contract and the laws: these are its positive dogmas. Its negative dogmas I would confine to one — intolerance, which is only congenial to the cults we have excluded.

Those who make a distinction between civil and theological intolerance are, in my opinion, mistaken. The two are inseparable. It is impossible to live in peace with those whom we believe damned; to love them would be to hate God who punishes them: we positively must either reclaim them or torment them. Wherever theological intolerance is admitted, it is impossible for it not to produce some civil effect:[10] as soon as it has produced it, the Sovereign ceases to be such, even in temporal concerns: the priests are from that time so absolutely masters that kings themselves are nothing more than their officers.

[9] When Cæsar was pleading the cause of Catiline, he endeavoured to establish the dogma of the mortality of the soul. Cato and Cicero, in the arguments they employed to confute him, did not reason as philosophers, but contented themselves with showing that Cæsar spoke like a bad citizen, and advanced a doctrine pernicious to the State. In fact, it was this that the Roman Senate was called upon to judge, and not a theological question.

[10] Marriage, for instance, is a civil contract and produces civil effects, without which it would be impossible for society even to subsist. Supposing that a body of clergy were to arrogate to themselves the exclusive right of permitting this act, a right which every intolerant religion must necessarily usurp, is it not then clear that, in establishing the authority of the Church in this respect, they injure that of the prince, the number of whose subjects will depend on what the clergy is willing to permit him? For the priest who can marry, or refuse to marry, people according as they shall or shall not profess such and such a doctrine, or in con-

Now that there neither is, nor can be any more, an exclusive national religion, all religions that tolerate others ought to be tolerated, so long as their dogmas discover nothing contradictory to the duties of a citizen. But those who dare to say: "Outside the Church there is no salvation," should be driven from the State, unless that State is the Church, and the prince the pontiff. Such a dogma is only suited to a theocratic government; in all others it is exceedingly pernicious. The very reason which it is said made Henry IV embrace the Roman religion is the one which should make any honest man renounce it, and particularly any prince who is capable of reason.

CHAPTER IX

CONCLUSION

AFTER HAVING ESTABLISHED the true principles of political right, and endeavoured to found the State on its proper basis, it remains to support it by its external relations, which comprehends the law of nations, commerce, the right of war, and of conquest, public right, leagues, negotiations, treaties, etc. But all this forms a new subject too vast for my circumscribed view, which I ought always to have confined within a narrower circle.

sideration of their admitting or rejecting such or such forms, or as they shall be more or less devout, may, by an artful and steady conduct, dispose of all inheritances, public employments, citizens, and even of the State itself, which could not subsist if by his management it should be peopled with none but bastards. But, say the favourers of the Church, the injured parties can appeal in consequence of this abuse: and the priest may be summoned, judged, and deprived of his revenues. What a pity! The clergy, with the little share they have, I will not say of courage, but of good sense, will pay no attention and go their way. They will calmly suffer appeals, summonses, decrees and deprivation of their benefices; and, in the end, will show themselves masters. This is, however, no great sacrifice to yield a little, when they are sure at last of carrying all before them. [This note was not contained in the first edition of the *Social Contract* (1762), but it was contained in editions secretly published during the same year.]

SELECTED BIBLIOGRAPHY

The student who wishes to learn more about Rousseau would do well to start with Rousseau's own works, beginning with the *Confessions* and *Emile*, and proceeding to his discourses *On the Arts and Sciences* and *On the Origin of Inequality*. The *Discourse on Political Economy*, Book V of *Emile*, and Rousseau's *Government of Poland* are especially recommended as collateral reading with *The Social Contract*.

Irving Babbitt . . *Rousseau and Romanticism* (Boston, 1919).

Bernard Bosanquet *The Philosophical Theory of the State* (London, 1899), Chapters 4–5.

Ernst Cassirer . . "Das Problem Jean-Jacques Rousseau," *Archiv für Geschichte der Philosophie*, XLI (1932).
Rousseau, Kant, Goethe (Princeton, 1945).

Alfred Cobban . . *Rousseau and the Modern State* (London, 1934).

E. Dreyfus-Brisac, ed., *Du Contrat Social* (Paris, 1896), Introduction.

Louis Ducros . . *Jean Jacques Rousseau* (Paris, 1908–1918).

Léon Duguit . . *Jean Jacques Rousseau, Kant et Hegel* (Paris, 1918).

Emile Faguet . . *La politique comparée de Montesquieu, Rousseau et Voltaire* (Paris, 1902).
Rousseau artiste (Paris, 1912).
Vie de Rousseau (Paris, 1911).

Charles W. Hendel . *Jean-Jacques Rousseau, Moralist* (London, 1934).

Harald Höffding . *Jean-Jacques Rousseau and His Philosophy* (New Haven, 1930).

René Hubert . . *Rousseau et l'encyclopédie* (Paris, 1928).

Jules Lemaître . . *Jean Jacques Rousseau* (New York, 1907).

Jacques Maritain . *Three Reformers: Luther, Descartes, Rousseau* (New York, 1929).

John Morley . . *Rousseau* (London, 1883).

Albert Schinz . . *La pensée de Jean-Jacques Rousseau* (Paris, 1929).

Norman L. Torrey . *Rousseau's Quarrel with Grimm and Diderot* (New Haven, 1943).

C. E. Vaughan, ed., *The Political Writings of Jean Jacques Rousseau* (Cambridge, 1915), Introduction.

Ernest H. Wright . *The Meaning of Rousseau* (Oxford, 1929).

INDEX